A TALENT
TO DECEIVE

CRIME FICTION BY ROBERT BARNARD

The Cherry Blossom Corpse
Bodies
Political Suicide
Fête Fatale
Out of the Blackout
Corpse in a Guilded Cage
School for Murder
The Case of the Missing Brontë
A Little Local Murder
Death and the Princess
Death by Sheer Torture
Death in a Cold Climate
Death of a Perfect Mother
Death of a Literary Widow
Death of a Mystery Writer

OTHER WRITINGS

Imagery and Theme in the Novels of Dickens
A Short History of English Literature

A
TALENT
TO
DECEIVE

An Appreciation of Agatha Christie

Revised and Updated

ROBERT BARNARD

THE MYSTERIOUS PRESS
New York   London

Printed in the United States of America
First Trade Paperback Printing: August 1987
10 9 8 7 6 5 4 3 2 1

Library of Congress Cataloging-in-Publication Data

Barnard, Robert.
    A talent to deceive.

    Reprint. Previously published: New York: Dodd,
Mead, c1980.
    Includes bibliographies.
    Includes index.
    1. Christie, Agatha, 1890–1976—Criticism and inter-
pretation.   2. Detective and mystery stories, English—
History and criticism.   I. Title.
PR6005.H66Z556   1987   823'.912   87-5515
ISBN 0-89296-911-3 (pbk) (U.S.A.)
        0-89296-912-1 (pbk) (Canada)

Contents

CONTENTS

VI
Strategies of Deception

VII
Three Prize Specimens

VIII
A Note about Detectives

IX
Counsel for the Defense

Appendices

I
Bibliography *(compiled by Louise Barnard)*

II
Short-Story Index *(compiled by Louise Barnard)*

III
Secondary Sources

CONTENTS

Preface

This appreciation of a writer who has probably given more sheer pleasure than any other in this century does not pretend to be literary criticism; still less is it intended as a contribution to the growing academic study of popular literature. It is written in the hope that some of those who "buy a Christie" for a train journey as automatically as they buy a ticket might also like to speculate a little on the reasons for her near-universal, apparently unfading appeal.

I found it impossible to write a book of this sort, dealing to a large extent with the kinds of deception Christie practices on her readers, without revealing solutions from time to time. I realize many readers will object to this, and can only plead that Christie did it herself: the solution to *Orient Express* is revealed in *Cards on the Table,* and no fewer than four of her earlier murderers are named in *Dumb Witness.* Most of my revelations of the culprit occur in chapters IV to VI, so the reader who has not read all the classic Christies may like to avoid these chapters until he has.

Since this is intended as a popular book, I have not burdened it with any apparatus of scholarly notes, page references, etc. However, I have given the source of a quote where it seemed the reader might want to follow it up. The bibliography, which is the work of my wife, will clear up any confusion about American and English titles. This bibliography is not intended to be comprehensive (an impossible task within a limited space), but to provide the main outlines of each book's publishing history. All the appendices are designed to help the Christie buff through the mountain of stuff she wrote, and to suggest some fruitful further reading.

I

Counsel for the Prosecution

Back in the 1940s, when the craze for detective stories was at its height, the critic Edmund Wilson recorded a note of dissent to the general chorus of praise and fascination. In a pair of articles written in 1944–45 he took as his starting point the general popularity of the detective story: the talk so often turned to them at parties that he felt excluded as a nonreader of them; people were continually recommending certain detective writers to his notice. Accordingly he had conscientiously plowed through the favorite writers of one or other of his friends and correspondents: Rex Stout ("sketchy and skimpy"), Dorothy L. Sayers ("one of the dullest books I have encountered in any field"), Ngaio Marsh ("unappetizing sawdust"), and Margery Allingham ("completely unreadable"). Many of the writers most commonly admired today passed before his beady gaze, including Raymond Chandler and Dashiell Hammett ("not much above . . . newspaper picture-strips"). They were all, he concluded, beneath contempt: the stories were childish in the extreme—ridiculous tissues of improbabilities; the characterization was at best conventional; the writing was dreadful beyond belief. There was literally nothing in the post-Doyle detective story that a man of cultivated literary taste could conscientiously take pleasure in.

This was all very well—and granted his point of view one might agree with most or all of his strictures. But he chose to call one of his essays on the subject "Who Cares Who Killed Roger Ackroyd?" and this is a question that ought to have given him furiously to think. Without having precise figures for that particular title, it is relevant to record that paperback Christies have sold well over two hundred million copies in the States alone; that her world sales are well over four hundred million; that she is the world's third-best-selling author—after Shakespeare and the Bible. An awful lot of people care who killed Roger Ackroyd. And this is the writer of whom Wilson said: "her writing is of a mawkishness and banality which seem to me literally impossible to read."

This incredible sales record is a success based entirely on the books themselves—it has owed nothing whatsoever to tie-ups with television or films (which have mostly been very bad)—and it is therefore in a different category from the success of several modern thriller and spy-story writers whose initial critical réclame is boosted by a film into a big popular sales boom. Year after year, come rain or shine, Agatha Christie delivered her manuscript to her publishers; year after year that book shot automatically to the top of the best-seller lists in Britain and the States, and usually stayed there for months. Thus, quite apart from the question of why detective stories appeal so widely, there is the additional question of what it was about Agatha Christie's books that put her streets ahead in public estimation of all the other practitioners of her debased craft.

And if Edmund Wilson shows in his essay that he does not understand the significance of the detective story's popularity, he also totally fails to face up to the question of the kind of audience it appeals to. Much more interesting in Christie's case than the brute force of sales statistics is the *kind* of popularity she seems to enjoy. I was lying on a beach in Italy a couple of summers ago, and next to me in a deck chair was an Italian lady in late middle age reading a book about la signorina Marple. Two days later I was walking through Tromsø, above the Arctic circle, and saw a teenage girl sitting in a deck chair, reading a book about frøken Marple. Agatha Christie has been translated into every language under the sun, and every nationality and age group finds something to respond to in her books. Eventually everyone seems to capitulate: in 1940 Russia called her books "A deliberate attempt by the Cripps-Bevin-Attlee-Churchill hyenas...to distract the attention of the masses from the machinations of the warmongers," but before very long she was appearing under the officially approved stamp of the state publishing house. No doubt she will shortly be found once again on the shelves of Chinese bookshops, as part of the Great Leap Backward.* One might expect such universality of appeal with the mythic simplicities of the Tarzan formula or the Western formula. But stories about English country houses and English villages? What do they have that goes so unerringly to the hearts and minds of Everyman and Everywoman?

For she not only bridges national and generational gaps; she seems to appeal equally to all class and intelligence brackets. No doubt her readership has been predominantly middle class, but of whom is this not true? Have Lawrence, Orwell or David Storey been eagerly devoured in the back streets of Bootle? It is true of any writer of books that deserve the name of books that he is read predominantly by the middle class. Agatha Christie's working-class readership was probably more numerous than that of any other popular writer, and she is said, not surprisingly, to be favored reading in Buckingham Palace.

Nor can this be shrugged off as success with the comparatively simple-minded. If she is read by miners, shop assistants and old-

---

*This prophecy was fulfilled almost as soon as it was written, with a massive release of Christie books on the Chinese market. It has been followed by a recent deal to show the BBC Miss Marple series. The reason given, as so often, is that Christie is useful in the teaching of the English language.

age pensioners, equally she is read—in spite of Edmund Wilson's superior sighs—by academics, politicians, scientists and artists. They would feel ashamed to sit on a train reading a Tarzan book; they would hide a James Bond inside a copy of the *Guardian;* but they wouldn't think twice about opening up a Christie. Again, the sort of book Christie writes may be intellectually negligible and socially irrelevant, yet it has stimulated some splendid satires and spoofs in the last few decades by writers as good as Dylan Thomas, Orton, Stoppard and Shaffer, as well as in earlier generations attracting practitioners of the quality of J. I. M. Stewart, C. Day Lewis and the Coles, who presumably saw in it a little more than a fast buck. There will always be dissentient voices like Wilson's —people who simply don't see what other people can enjoy in the detective story as a genre, and are therefore determined to poison their pleasure. But one catches in the aggrieved defensiveness of their tone the realization that they are in a minority—and quite a small minority at that. As far as it is in one writer to be, Christie's appeal (like Dickens's) is universal, cutting across every possible barrier of race, color, class and intelligence.

The question "Who Cares Who Killed Roger Ackroyd?" is therefore a simple one: if the answer is not "everybody," it is as near to it as any writer in our time has come. But of course mere popularity will not still the voices of those who, like Edmund Wilson, quite simply find her books trashy—any more than most people would alter their opinion of the James Bond books because they had seen the sales figures. The charges usually leveled against Agatha Christie's books are perfectly serious, even damaging, and though—as I hope to show—they seem to me to be based on a fundamental misunderstanding of the sort of book she was writing, they need to be set down in full and aired. To do this with at least an appearance of fairness, I shall adopt for the present the role of Counsel for the Prosecution.

The first and commonest charge against the Christie books is that the characterization is rudimentary in the extreme—much

more so than in most of her rivals. In the novels of her classic
period (which for the purposes of this book I shall take to be
roughly 1925–50) she has a stock repertoire of characters whom
she wheels on and off stage to perform their stock gestures: the
pompous and boring Anglo-Indian colonel; the acid-tongued
spinster; the vulgar, newly rich businessman; the egotistical actor
or actress; the ne'er-do-well young man. It is almost as if she had
a pack of cards with a series of types baldly characterized, and
before beginning a new book she shuffled and dealt herself ten or
twelve to make up a cast-list of suspects. Very occasionally she
brings off something with a degree of psychological depth: the
womanizing artist in *Five Little Pigs* [U.S. *Murder in Retrospect*], and the
women who surround him; the spoiled young rich boy in *Towards
Zero* [U.S. *Come and Be Hanged*]. But even here the characterization
hardly rises above the level of a quite ordinary conventional novel.

And almost all these stock outlines are drawn from a tiny part
of the complex class structure of between-the-wars Britain. They
are middle-middle to upper-middle class: army men, clergymen
(rural, never from the higher reaches), men from the colonies,
country gentry, *successful* (or long-established) doctors or dentists.
And, of course, the women who depend on them—which is what
they do in Christie, and what (as she makes clear in the *Autobiography*) she thought they ought to do. As a cross-section of society
it is, to say the least, inadequate. Have the working classes no
murders ingenious enough to bear investigation? And even when
she goes outside England for her locales, the characterization var-
ies very little. These are books about monied tourists, of various
nationalities. In general, we are watching a leisured class, and if her
characters have a profession, we almost never see them at it. About
the only *work* ever done in a Christie novel is archeology—hardly
the most representative form of labor, sweated or otherwise.

In her last years, it is true, she tried to broaden her range and
include new social types of the 'fifties and 'sixties—coffee-bar
society, mini-skirted girls, disturbed young men of dubious social

background. But the results are seldom entirely convincing. We are never left in any doubt that this is an old person interpreting the younger generation for the benefit of other old people—trying to be fair, giving them the benefit of the doubt. And sometimes these efforts are downright embarrassing.

Most of these books take place in an eternal fairyland disguised as an English village. As with the class components of the novels, it is in fact a *segment* of a village, not a full picture: it comprises the manorhouse, the vicarage and a selection of genteel houses of various sizes. Poverty, dirt and disease are dealt with in a throwaway subordinate clause. There is not even any feel of village life or village architecture—the insipidity of the writing sees to that. These villages are totally interchangeable, they are generalized and flat. Similarly London has no feel of London, Mesopotamia has no feel of Mesopotamia. We are in an eternal no-man's land.

The inadequacy of her settings necessarily ties in with the inadequacy of her writing. "If I could write like Elizabeth Bowen, Muriel Spark or Graham Greene, I would jump to high heaven with delight, but I know I can't," she writes in her *An Autobiography*. No indeed. At best she can manage no more than a plain, journeyman's style, rather loose grammatically, totally lacking in vividness or any ability to use language in a pictorial way. Her books are much analyzed by foreign linguists studying the behavior of this or that grammatical phenomenon, but it is not easy to see why: perhaps she writes with such a simple vocabulary that even they can understand her. Nor is her writing often funny. It may be entertaining, jolly, but it almost never rises to wit. Sometimes, to be fair, she can cunningly insert a brief, sharp piece of observation or comment. Here, for example, is Poirot in *The Mystery of the Blue Train* meditating on the dilemma of the heroine, torn between a dull, safe, respectable young man, and the inevitable handsome ne'er-do-well: "Moral worth is not romantic. It is appreciated, however, by widows."

But the occasional sharp point such as this is lost in the suet pudding of her habitual style. Other parts of the same book (which admittedly she thought the worst she ever wrote) are stylistically so dreadful as to seem like parody:

> The Comte de la Roche had just finished *déjeuner,* consisting of an *omelette fines herbes,* an *entrecôte Béarnaise,* and a *Savarin au Rhum.* Wiping his fine black moustache delicately with his table napkin, the Comte rose from the table. He passed through the salon of the villa, noting with appreciation the few *objets d'art* which were scattered carelessly about. The Louis XV snuff-box, the satin shoe worn by Marie Antoinette, and other historical trifles that were part of the Comte's *mise en scène.*

Agatha Christie, the reader will not be surprised to learn, studied music for a time in Paris.

And here, for the moment, the voice of the Counsel for the Prosecution may be allowed to die away. He will have some stern things to say in the next chapter or two on Christie's social and racial attitudes, for these are—perhaps rightly—points which are often fastened upon by those who find her repellent and those who admit her fascination against what they feel to be their better judgment. The burden of the Prosecution case as a whole, then, is that these books are worthless: trivial, dated, class-bound, socially and intellectually dead. Their appeal is to the lowest kind of mind, to which any kind of puzzle, however feeble, is better than no puzzle at all. It is the sort of public vice that is best ignored, in the hope that it will go away.

But one more thing needs to be said about Edmund Wilson and the rest of the voices raised against the English detective story of the traditional type (voices greatly reinforced, in recent years, by the cult for Chandler and Hammett). For in the end, as we have seen, they cannot avoid admitting that it is confoundedly popular —so popular that one sometimes feels it is the popularity that is unforgivable. Today there are many practicing detective-story writers anxious to state their belief that crime stories of this type are "fossils." And yet, and yet. . . . Detective stories of this rarefied kind may not be *written* in any great number today, but goodness they are *read.* Any bookseller knows that the paperbacks that sell are not the modern psychological crime stories but the traditional whodunnits of Christie, Marsh et al. The generation of crime writers that came after Christie—the Innes, Crispin, Symons, Michael Gilbert generation—made little impact on the mass public. The newer generation—Ruth Rendell, P. D. James—is only just beginning to dent the public preference for the "fossils." So dated, so irrelevant, and yet so compulsive, still, today. . . . Why?

Edmund Wilson came up with a couple of explanations. On the one hand, he said that in the years between the wars everyone was ridden by a pervasive sense of guilt and a fear of impending disaster. The detective formula was comforting because it involved an infallible person who could spot the guilt and rid the community of the sinner. Wilson, writing in 1944, seems to have hoped that in the changed situation of the postwar world, the detective story would pack its bags and leave the house of fiction by the back door. But though the social, political and ideological state of the world has changed and changed again in the last thirty-odd years, the whodunnit is still with us, shelf after shelf, on every station bookstall.

Even Wilson was not too happy with this explanation, it seems, because in his second article he came up with something else—an only half-humorous explanation that these books were a narcotic, something that readers got hooked on and then tried shamelessly to spread as a habit among their innocent friends. And doubtless there is an element of addiction in the reading of detective fiction, though there are few addicts who are so hooked as to devote themselves exclusively to that particular stimulus. But what is the nature of the original appeal? Here is a genre with few of the more titillating and debasing aspects of modern popular reading—eroticism, sentimentality, even violence are sparingly used or totally absent (for the violence of a detective story is of an academic, nonthrilling kind). Simply to call it a drug is to go no way toward explaining why people need it, and what they find in it that satisfies their cravings.

There is one further possible explanation. This is that the traditional whodunnit is a popular fictional form that is viable, satisfying and stimulating in an entirely worthy way, that it appeals to and satisfies sides of our nature not catered for by other popular forms, and that Agatha Christie is a supremely gifted practitioner of this—we won't say art, but—craft. Farfetched, perhaps, but the reader might like to keep this possibility in mind in the pages that follow.

II

"Their Aim Is World Domination"

Of the eleven titles which Agatha Christie published in the 'twenties, only five or six are works of detection. The rest are what, for want of a better title, we must call "thrillers." They are in fact extravaganzas of international espionage and worldwide conspiracy. The villains are not just murderers; they are monomaniacs whose aim—like that of the Big Four in the book of that title—is "world domination." We are closer, then, to the world of James Bond than to that of St. Mary Mead, though it seems to us, with the hindsight of a post-Bond generation, to be a world of rather amateur investigators and unmechanized villains. Not only Fleming but the daily newspapers as well have accustomed us to viewing espionage in terms of fantastic gadgetry and hideous professional expertise.

These thrillers, we can now see, represent something of a false start for Agatha Christie: she was not yet quite sure where her

real talent lay. In the first part of this period she was a young
and apparently carefree married woman writing for pocket
money; in the later part she was a deeply unhappy and disturbed
woman with a breakdown and a ruined marriage in her past,
hardly able to settle down to concentrated writing. These thrillers were easier to do than the brand of detective story she was
beginning to perfect. In *An Autobiography* she defined them as
"the light-hearted thriller which is particularly pleasant to do,"
and distinguished them from "the intricate detective story with
an involved plot which is technically interesting and requires a
great deal of work." It was a form she returned to from time to
time throughout her long career—for example, in *N or M* (1941),
Destination Unknown (1954) [U.S. *So Many Steps to Death*] and *Passenger to Frankfurt* (1970).

Almost always with disastrous results. The ease with which
these stories could be cobbled together shows all too clearly.
Though they are admired in America, where (incredibly) *Passenger to Frankfurt* set the final seal on her best-seller status, in Britain these are the Christies that are usually shrugged off as an
obvious embarrassment: even the *Times Literary Supplement*, in a
generous and enthusiastic tribute on her eightieth birthday,
could only manage to give that particular thriller a passing
"alas." What makes them intermittently interesting is the fact
that *because* she was relaxing, writing lighthearted nonsense, her
guard was down. In the detective stories (as we shall see later)
there is little or nothing that can be pinned down as a Christie
opinion or a Christie taste. She is infinitely more circumspect
than Dorothy L. Sayers. In the thrillers, on the other hand, she
sometimes gives herself away.

The years which saw the first publication of these early thrillers,
the 'twenties, were far from the years of peace and reversion to
Edwardian tranquillity that many people of Mrs. Christie's class
had hoped for. After the terrible years of slaughter, smug normal-

ity was not so easily regained, and to many this was no bad thing. These were the years which saw the consolidation of the Russian Revolution and the widening ripples of consequences it had for Western Europe; of the Irish "troubles"; of the first Labour government, and the General Strike. All these things are reflected in the early Christie thrillers, and the last, the General Strike, is repeatedly anticipated in the novels published before it occurred. What is notable is the *way* these things are reflected: we seem to be viewing them through a glass, crookedly.

We seem to be viewing them, in fact, through the eyes of one of those elderly characters in early Waugh—puzzled and enraged by what the world has become, postulating high-sounding generalizations to explain the new world struggling into existence around him, which he neither likes nor understands, vaguely looking for some conspiracy theory that will enable him to shrug off personal responsibility. Some such conspiracy, in fact, is behind the events in most of these thrillers: it aims to control events in Britain by using the labor unions, the Sinn Fein leaders and the occasional treacherous Member of Parliament. And not just in Britain either: Agatha Christie is much taken by the idea that "Lenin and Trotsky were mere puppets whose every action was dictated by another's brain"—and since much of the political unrest in the Empire and the labor unrest in the States is the work of the same brain, there is really hardly anywhere left where Civilization as We Know It is unthreatened.

In this struggle the British antiespionage organization cannot afford to be politically neutral. It is on the side of the government (provided it is right-wing, which unfortunately you couldn't be absolutely sure about in the 'twenties) and prepared to act against the machinations of the opposition. Which in fact is what a lot of people have suspected about MI5 all along. Here is Mr. Carter of "Intelligence" giving a round-up of the international scene to a breathless and sympathetic Tommy and Tuppence at the beginning of *The Secret Adversary:*

> "[T]hat document undoubtedly implicates a number of our statesmen whom we cannot afford to have discredited in any way at the present moment. As a party cry for Labour it would be irresistible, and a Labour Government at this juncture would, in my opinion be a grave disability for British trade, but that is a mere nothing to the *real* danger. . . ."

And he goes on to give the pair all the dreadful details of the "Bolshevist influence at work behind the present labour unrest," the "Bolshevist gold" which is "pouring into this country for the specific purpose of procuring a revolution." He then goes on to describe the adversary they are up against in chilling tones: "The Bolshevists are behind the labour unrest—but this man is *behind the Bolshevists.*" He was also, it seems, behind "most of the peace propaganda during the war." In a few pages Christie manages to at least graze quite a remarkable number of targets, and to warm the hearts of every Torquay deck-chair dozer of the time.

No doubt we are taking all this a little too seriously. Agatha Christie remarks in *An Autobiography* that thrillers are much alike:

> All that alters is the Enemy. There is an international gang *à la* Moriarty—provided first by the Germans, the "Huns" of the first war; then the Communists, who in turn were succeeded by the Fascists. We have the Russians, we have the Chinese, we go back to the international gang again, and the Master Criminal wanting world supremacy is always with us.

But what is really remarkable about the political background to these thrillers is that, though Agatha Christie was a young and not unintelligent woman when she wrote them, we feel ourselves here not in a 'twenties world, but in a 'nineties one—a world where the

Latin male could be called a dago without apology, embarrassment or implied criticism of the speaker, where Chinese are inevitably impassive and fiendishly cruel, where foreigners of all kinds are either comic or suspicious.* Reading the early Christie thrillers gives one the impression that the modern world has caught up with their middle-middle-class characters, but that they have scarcely caught up with it. Their attitudes and ideals are still aggressively Edwardian, or even older.

The earliest of these novels, *The Secret Adversary* (1922) is the first to feature Tommy and Tuppence, everybody's least favorite Christie sleuths, whom she unwisely resurrected for a few geriatric trots at the end of her career. This is certainly one of the best of their adventures, though that is not to rate it very high. Here they foil the plans of the villain, "Mr. Brown," who is apparently already in charge of Russia but is unreasonably sighing for fresh fields to conquer. His ambitions for seizing control of England hinge on a projected General Strike which he is stage-managing, though the Labour leaders believe it to be of their own making. Thanks to the two adventurers, he is prevented from discrediting the British government by revealing their attempts to sign a treaty with Germany during the war. Thus Labour Day passes off without incident, England is saved for Lloyd George and Bonar Law, and even the Labour leaders are revealed to have hearts of patriotic gold:

Sensational hints of a Labour *coup d'état* were freely reported. The Government said nothing. It knew and was prepared. There were rumours of dissension among the Labour leaders. They were not of one mind. The more far-seeing among them realized that what they proposed might well be a death-blow to the

---

*To be fair, a similar set of preconceptions seems to lie behind the Bond novels, allied with a much less endearing view of life. And where Christie's prejudices were the common currency of popular writers of her time, Fleming's seem to be a hectic and anachronistic playing on dated taboos.

England that at heart they loved. They shrank from the starvation and misery a general strike would entail, and were willing to meet the Government half-way. But behind them were subtle, insistent forces at work, urging the memories of old wrongs, deprecating the weakness of half-and-half measures, fomenting misunderstandings.

As the above quotation suggests, if we take the political assumptions of these books seriously, then the young Mrs. Christie was, to put it politely, a most apolitical person. Alternatively she was pandering to the prejudices of her imagined audience with a few warmed-over *Daily Telegraph* clichés. Certainly she is in these books remarkably self-revealing, compared to her detective-story self. Take for example *The Secret of Chimneys*—perhaps the best of the bunch, and a very jolly romp. The obvious enjoyment of the writer seems to lower her defenses still further. The plot concerns the throne of Herzoslovakia,* and is a farrago of comic foreigners and international jewel thieves. There are one or two pleasant characters, including a reluctant lord and a cleverly caricatured politician who can never adjust his voice to speaking outside the House.

The fly in the ointment for present-day readers is the number of remarks with unpleasant racial or political overtones. 'Dagos will be dagos,' remarks the hero cheerfully to his friend, and 'any name's good enough for a dago.' Much good unclean fun is had with the All-British Syndicate which aims to achieve oil concessions in Herzoslovakia and is run by someone called Hermann Isaacstein, charmingly nicknamed by the bright young central characters 'Fat Ikey' and 'Noseystein'. We are still in the era when a novelist can make the flesh creep by references to 'Hebraic people, yellow-faced financiers in city offices.' These

---

*In common with many central European states this country seems to have suffered from disputed boundaries, and in *The Labours of Hercules* (1947) and *Hallowe'en Party* (1969) it is named as Herzogovinia.

references were never removed in later editions, any more than the even more offensive allusions in Dorothy Sayers have disappeared from Gollancz editions to this day. Christie's American publishers, however, have silently edited them out, which may conceivably be good for race relations but is bad for the social historian.

It is fair to add, though, that Poirot, a cosmopolitan figure, has Jewish friends both at the beginning and end of his career (Joseph Aarons in *The Mystery of the Blue Train* and Solomon Levy in *Hallowe'en Party*) and that things did change over the years. In the novels of the 'twenties one can be fairly sure that any Jewish character will be ridiculed, abused or rendered sinister. Even as late as the early 'thirties Christie can perpetrate a remark such as: 'He's a Jew, of course, but a frightfully decent one.' However, as she records in her *Autobiography*, about that date she had a meeting in the Near East with a German Director of Antiquities whom she describes as ideally kind, gentle and considerate—until the mention of Jews, at which 'his face changed' and he said: 'They should be exterminated. Nothing else will really do but that.' The remark came apparently as a complete shock: 'It was the first time I had come across any hint of what was to come later from Germany.' A more politically sensitive person might have sensed the rise of organized anti-Semitism earlier; might even have expressed shame at her own unthinking acceptance of repulsive attitudes. But at any rate from that date offensive references to Jews cease in her novels. In later books Jews and attitudes towards them are part and parcel of one of her cleverest tricks: to use the reader's prejudices and preconceptions *against* him, as an instrument of his own deception.

The xenophobic references in the early thrillers are in fact consistent with the general contempt displayed for those outside the charmed circle of the central characters. One of the bright young men at the center of *The Secret of Chimneys* disguises himself as an out-of-work itinerant, but he is spotted at once by the delightful heroine as "more pleasing than the usual specimen of London's unemployed." Such men were (as Christie notes in *An Autobiography*) a depressingly familiar sight to thinking people at the time—men who had miraculously survived the slaughter and come home to poverty and idleness. In this book Christie appears to see them as no more than fraudulent nuisances. This one carries a pamphlet called "Why Did I Serve My Country?" which apparently is to be regarded as an impertinent question. To take such a tone in the 'twenties must seem to the modern reader both crass and discreditable. Hardly less distasteful is another dismissal of one outside the charmed circle—a remark by the charming heroine when she wonders where she has seen the governess before:

> "I certainly know her face quite well—in that vague way one does know governesses and companions and people one sits opposite to in trains. It's awful, but I never really look at them properly. Do you?"

It is as if *Jane Eyre* had never been written.

The only thing that can save these extravaganzas is lightness of touch. *The Secret of Chimneys* has it, and so have the early chapters of *The Man in the Brown Suit*, which has something rare in Christie at any time—a good joke:

> "Is this your first visit to Africa?" [The heroine is talking to a missionary.]
> "To South Africa, yes. But I have worked for the last two years among the cannibal tribes in the interior of East Africa."
> "How thrilling! Have you had many narrow escapes?"
> "Escapes?"
> "Of being eaten, I mean?"
> "You should not treat sacred subjects with levity, Miss Beddingfield."

"I didn't know cannibalism was a sacred subject," I retorted, stung.

The Seven Dials Mystery has a preposterous solution but along the way there are several delightful things in the Wodehousian manner (Mrs. Christie testified to her admiration for the magician of Blandings Castle). There is, for example, Lady Coote with her Mrs. Siddons airs and her habit of leaning over and looking straight at her opponents' cards at bridge, and the pompous politician resurrected from *Chimneys*. But such successes are intermittent, and the main interest of these books is in their unzipped revelation of the young Agatha Christie's attitudes. Of course, these sentiments are almost invariably put into the mouths of characters, but surely one is not mistaken in reading into the words of Superintendent Battle in *Seven Dials* a Brodie-esque contempt for the then prime minister which is the author's own:

"I never have thought much of the motto 'Safety First.' In my opinion half the people who spend their lives avoiding being run over by buses had much better be run over and put safely out of the way. They're no good."*

This is all of a piece with other attitudes in the early thrillers. Behind them, never openly expressed, probably not even conscious, is a nostalgia for the heyday of Empire, for men who carved fortunes for themselves from virgin lands, for rough on-the-spot justice, and fist-law. It is not for nothing that South Africa and South Africans feature so prominently and are described so glowingly in these stories, while Australia, which seems for Christie to have lost the pioneer spirit, is colored far more soberly and seems the refuge or place of origin of a great

*Cf. *Autobiography* (Fontana) p. 432: "I have never refrained from doing anything on the grounds of security." See also *Cards on the Table*, chapter 13, where Battle's sentiment is repeated almost word for word.

many of her more shady characters. The young Christie's ideal statesman, one would guess, was much more likely to be Rhodes** than the timid time-servers who led the British Conservatives in the 'twenties and 'thirties.

But at the same time as she was giving herself away in these books Agatha Christie was training herself to write in a very different vein. The other sort of book that she knew she could write was, as she insists many times in *An Autobiography*, much more difficult: it involved great discipline, self-abnegation and an almost abstract, mathematical approach to creative writing. As a thriller writer she was never better than second-rate. As a crime novelist, writing at the height of the crossword puzzle and jigsaw craze, she hit on their fictional equivalent and laid the foundations for a career of unparalleled reader-appeal. She was finding the road to Mayhem Parva.

**Her attitude to the white colonies is at least less embarrassing than Conan Doyle's in the conclusion of "The Adventure of the Three Students," where the student who has just been caught cheating is dismissed to a career in the Rhodesian *police force*—where, in the words of Sherlock Holmes, "I trust a bright future awaits you."

III

The Road to Mayhem Parva

In 1917, when Agatha Christie was mixing poisons and writing her first detective story, Sherlock Holmes was making *His Last Bow.* It was not, of course, to prove his last bow, any more than his Final Problem had been his final problem. It is easy to forget that the young Christie and the elderly Doyle were writing detection simultaneously, and that Poirot first appeared in the shadow of the incomparable Holmes.

To the young writer of the time who aimed at a popular market the example of Doyle must have been at once inspiring and intimidating. The magnitude of his success was incontrovertible, and manifested itself in concrete worldly terms: he could virtually name his own price for a Holmes story; he had risen almost overnight from a poverty-stricken doctor with a dwindling practice to a country gentleman, knighted for services to his country; he had stood for Parliament, and his voice was listened to in all manner of matters normally considered beyond a novelist's competence.

But the sheer range of his achievement in the popular sphere must also have been frightening. He had dabbled in science fiction, adventure, historical romance, humorous narrative, and everything had turned to gold. Nor had this been done by any lowering of quality or pandering to his market. It is often alleged that Holmes was never quite the same after his resurrection in 1902— that something went out of him after that duel over the Reichenbach Falls. In support of this contention he is accused of becoming less addicted to cocaine and more chivalrous to women—odd reasons, surely. In fact, *The Return of Sherlock Holmes* contains quite as many first-rate stories as the earlier volumes, and it is only right at the end, with *The Casebook,* that some diminution of quality becomes noticeable. In general Conan Doyle was justified in his confidence in the even quality of the Holmes stories:

> I was determined, now that I had no longer the excuse of absolute pecuniary pressure, never again to write anything which was not as good as I could possibly make it, and therefore I would not write a Holmes story without a worthy plot and without a problem which interested my own mind. . . . I have never, or hardly ever, forced a story.

To the modern reader, unfailingly captivated by the old spell, this seems no less than the truth.

Like many another young writer, Agatha Christie's first reaction to success was to copy it. She may have unconsciously taken the name of her detective from Mrs. Belloc Lowndes, but the relationship Poirot–Hastings–Japp is essentially a replica of the relationship Holmes–Watson–Lestrade, even down to quite small details of treatment. It is not identical, of course. Watson, in spite of the critics, is not a stupid man. We never feel contempt for him, for he *is* the average reader, neither more nor less intelligent. Only when Doyle's touch momentarily falters do we understand more than he does. Hastings, on the other hand, even we can perceive to be monumentally dim. Then again, the contempt inherent in Holmes's treatment of Watson ("Excellent Watson! You are scintillating this evening") is foreign to Poirot–Hastings, and we get, instead, something gentler, something of a benevolent tolerance by Poirot of Hastings's imbecilities. On one occasion Holmes, after witnessing a display of stupidity on the part of a university don, remarks: "Watson, I have always done you an injustice. There are others." The suave brutality of this is outside Christie's range, perhaps outside her nature, and in general the Holmes–Watson relationship is much more complex, more discomfiting than her version. She softens it. In later books she also vulgarizes it.

Such a stricture, however, hardly applies to the first book that features the pair, her debut novel *The Mysterious Affair at Styles.* Subsequently she found that she had inherited a relationship pattern which she could neither develop nor make her own. She therefore repeated Doyle's effects and they became cruder and cruder, so that on the whole the reader is grateful when Hastings is banished to Argentina and the void is filled, when the occasion demands a foil for Poirot, by his secretary and valet. In *Styles,* however, Christie is both writing more carefully than she sometimes did later on, and establishing the Poirot–Hastings partnership more delicately than one would expect from its later treatment. There is nothing mechanical here: Hastings's stupidity is not caricatured, and Poirot is given some depth, is less a figure with catch-phrases and oddities duly paraded. The humor has a dash of subtlety to it, as in the following conversation concerning the black beard hidden in the fancy-dress chest:

"Who put it in the chest, I wonder?"

"Someone with a good deal of intelligence," remarked Poirot drily. "You realize that he chose the one place in the house to hide it where its presence would not be remarked? Yes, he is intelligent. But we must be more intelligent. We must be so intelligent that he does not suspect us of being intelligent at all."

I acquiesced.

"There, *mon ami,* you will be of great assistance to me."

I was pleased with the compliment. . . .

In general *The Mysterious Affair at Styles* is a considerable achievement for a first-off author. The country-house-party murder is a stereotype in the detective-story genre which Christie makes no great use of. Not her sort of occasion, at least later in life, and perhaps not really her class. The family party is much more in her line, and this is what we have here. This is one of the few Christies anchored in time and space: we are in Essex, during the First World War. The family is kept together under one roof by the exigencies of war and of a matriarch demanding rather than tyrannical—not one of her later splendid monsters, but a sympathetic and lightly shaded characterization. If the lifestyle of the family still seems to us lavish, even wasteful, nevertheless we have a half sense that we are witnessing the beginning of the end of the Edwardian summer, that the era of country-house living has entered its final phase. Christie takes advantage of this end-of-an-era feeling in several ways: while she uses the full range of servants and their testimony, a sense of decline, of breakup is evident; feudal attitudes exist, but they crack easily. The marriage of the matriarch with a mysterious nobody is the central out-of-joint event in an intricate web of subtle changes. The family is lightly but effectively characterized, and on the outskirts of the story are the villagers, the small businessmen, and the surrounding farmers—the nucleus of Mayhem Parva.

It is, too, a very clever story, with clues and red herrings falling thick and fast. We are entering the age when plans of the house were an indispensable aid to the aspirant solver of detective stories, and when cleverness was more important than suspense. But here we come to a problem that Agatha Christie had not yet solved, for cleverness over the long length easily becomes exhausting, and too many clues tend to cancel each other out, as far as reader interest is concerned. These were problems that Conan

Doyle never satisfactorily overcame, but which Christie would. If one read only Conan Doyle one would think the detective formula unsuited to the longer length. If one read only Agatha Christie, on the other hand, one would think it unsuited to the short story. This is illustrated vividly in her first collection of stories, *Poirot Investigates* (1924), where the Poirot–Hastings relationship first becomes crude and mechanical, and where similar tricks are tried over and over again. It is significant that even in later years, when her hand became rather surer, most of her successful short stories were ones that she subsequently found could be enlarged to a film or a play or, in one case, where the basic idea could be reused in a full-length story ("Triangle at Rhodes" and *Evil under the Sun*). What *Styles* and *Murder on the Links* prove is that her adaptation of the formula to the longer length was a conscious matter of trial and error, of encountering problems and solving them. It is safe to say that if she were using the plot of *Styles* later she would halve the number of clues and ambiguities, and pace the story better. Tightness of construction is essential to the appeal of the detective story: if the plot does not move fast before the murder, it certainly should after it. Here too much time passes (what was Poirot *doing,* we ask ourselves?), the scene changes to London, a quite unnecessary trial takes place (caused by Poirot's tenderhearted desire to save a marriage) and in general the interest is dissipated. In the process one of Christie's best ideas—based on the fact that a man cannot be tried twice for the same crime—goes for very little, though it lies behind one of her later successes, the short story, radio play, stage play and film *Witness for the Prosecution.*

The setting of *Murder on the Links* is very different, and all her life Christie liked to alternate the more cosy, domestic books with something more exotic or metropolitan (the wisdom of which was proved at the end of her life when film companies became interested in the more cosmopolitan stories as the basis for films laden with star names who apparently could not be fitted into the Mayhem Parva background). Here we are in France, a country Agatha

Christie felt fairly confident about, having studied there before the First World War. The *Mon Dieu*s and the *Sacré tonnerre*s fall even thicker and faster than in the other Poirot stories. Here the pacing is much better. We get only one debilitating trip out of the French milieu, the story is fast and varied, and there is a new, more intelligent stooge for Poirot in the French policeman Giraud (while Hastings has an unlikely love affair). Generally it is clear that Christie is getting her powers as a storyteller well under control. The drawback is that in the exuberance of youth she is again overgenerous with her ingenuity, strewing clues with the carelessness of one who does not realize that she has fifty years of reader-deception ahead of her. The cleverness may have seemed to her early readers staggering, but the modern reader is by the end too punch-drunk to react to the surprise solution, which in any case is one of those overingenious ones she periodically indulged in. Another interesting drawback to the success of the novel with modern readers is a pair of lovers whose language is quite gloriously Victorian: "Nothing can part us now, beloved. The last obstacle to our union is removed." We are, we realize, on the hinge between two distinct ages. All in all, *Links* does not quite prepare us for the sort of disciplined success Christie achieved with her next true detective story, *The Murder of Roger Ackroyd.*

As everyone knows, it was with *Ackroyd* in 1926 that Agatha Christie's reputation was made, and her position among the foremost crime writers in this so-called Golden Age of crime became assured and indisputable. The reasons for this success we shall say more about in the next chapter. Our interest in it here is that with *Ackroyd* and her next major success, *The Murder at the Vicarage,* she established the typical milieu for a Christie detective story—the small English village to which critics, following Colin Watson, have given the generic name of Mayhem Parva.

The world of Mayhem Parva, like the world of Lady Dedlock —heroine of one of the earliest and still one of the best detective stories—is not a large world. . . . There is much good in it, there are many good and true people in it; it has its appointed place. But the evil of it is, that it is a world wrapped up in too much jeweller's cotton and fine wool. . . . It is a deadened world, and somewhat unhealthy for want of air. [Dickens, *Bleak House,* chapter 2]

It is a world shut off from the political and social preoccupations of the day. It cares little about what happens in London, and Europe might not exist, for all it cares. It is a world on which the nineteenth century has made little impact, and which accepts the twentieth only slowly and grumblingly. Though one feels the author imagines it in her own West Country, it owes more to *Cranford* than to Hardy. Here the old outnumber the young, and tradition wins small victories over innovation. The inhabitants of Mayhem Parva play bridge, and garden and go to church. They approve of self-help, self-control and capital punishment. They disapprove of Socialism, the modern woman and contemporary literature (which they associate with filth and poems without capital letters). They are doctors and lawyers, maiden ladies and retired capitalists, army men and ex-colonists. They are led spiritually by the vicar, and socially by the squire and his relations. They are all *very* aware of their proper stations.

The village itself is not atmospherically described. Agatha Christie wastes no fine writing on it. One may do for all:

Wychwood . . . consists mainly of its one principal street. There were shops, small Georgian houses, prim and aristocratic, with whitened steps and polished knockers, there were picturesque cottages with flower gardens. There was an inn, the Bells and Motley, standing a little back from the street. There was a village green and a duck pond, and presiding over them a dignified Georgian house. . . . [*Murder Is Easy* (U.S. *Easy to Kill*), chapter 3]

There is no sentimental commitment to place any more than there is any to the characters; the flat style enforces detachment.

In the 'fifties and the 'sixties change comes more quickly to Mayhem Parva: council houses are built; well-bred people take in paying guests; more and more rich vulgarians take over the manor-houses. But somehow the old life goes on: the same sort of people play bridge together; vicars remain unworldly and absentminded; the cleaning lady moves in with Miss Marple and proves much more feudal in her devotion than the little girls from the orphanage of yore. And perhaps, in this, Agatha Christie seizes on an essential truth—the survivability of the English middle class.

In the creation of Mayhem Parva, as in so much else, Christie got many hints from Conan Doyle. The Dartmoor setting of *The Hound of the Baskervilles* is too wild and desolate to fit easily under the Mayhem Parva heading, but many features of that book are adapted to Christie's own use in her village murders: the local doctor, the well-heeled eccentric, the mysterious outsiders with the ambiguous relationship (brother and sister? husband and wife?). Even the escaped convict on the fringes of the story is later pressed into service for *The Sittaford Mystery* [U.S. *Murder at Hazelmoor*].

Doyle's setting certainly isn't cozy, though, and this is the word which has most often been used to describe Christie's villages and the sort of detective story which is set there. They have been contrasted with the more fluid, vital, dangerous settings used by American crime writers. Here we have a stable social order, with the squire setting the tone for the village as a whole, a selection of the most respectable middle-class professions to establish the gentility of the place, and beneath these a largely voiceless lower class of agricultural and domestic workers, who can be called on to play small character parts in dialect at the author's will. Murder is a disruption of this stability, a threat to a God-ordained stability which the detective eradicates. As George Grella maintains in his article "Murder and Manners":

[Poirot's] short stature, his pomposity, his avuncular goodness and his foreign, otherworldly air, place him with the kindly elves of the fairytale. . . . Poirot, naturally, always employs his magic for good purposes, insuring that the fabric of society will be repaired after the temporary disruption of murder.

At the end divine order is restored, and the future is as sunny as on the last page of an early Dickens novel.

It is tempting to see the books like this. No doubt many readers read them like this, and one can't entirely go against the general testimony of readers. Nevertheless, it is as well to remember that horror stories tend to lull their readers with coziness to increase the shock impact of the horror. Much of the "coziness" of detective stories is really a matter of *contrast* with the violence and death that is to intrude on this world. And then, the blanket dismissal (or praise) of these books as "cozy" does not really correspond to the facts of an Agatha Christie village-murder mystery or the impression it makes on a careful reader. For example, such a view sees the murderer, and probably the victim too, as discordant elements in the general harmony which must be expelled in order to restore peace. But the whole basis of Miss Marple's detective ability is that murder is *not* an isolated crime: that parallels lower on the scale of moral turpitude can be found over and over again in the short and simple annals of village life. These parallels serve a similar function to the famous cases of Sherlock Holmes which are cited by Watson but never chronicled. They titillate the reader's interest. But puzzling crimes may be presumed to be part of a professional detective's life, whereas the parallels that Miss Marple cites establish in the reader's mind the uneasy sense that beneath the surface calm of village life there lurks a seething lava of crimes, sins, oddities and other potential disruptions—of which murder is only the most serious example. "We are not used to mysteries in St. Mary Mead" says the narrator of the first Miss Marple story—but surely that must be the misstatement of the century. For even within the dramatized action of the Mayhem Parva novels themselves, murder is seldom an isolated crime. Agatha Christie criticized *The Murder at the Vicarage* for having too many subplots, but it is fairly typical in having an awful lot going on apart from murder: adultery, theft, impersonation, and so on. Blackmail is a common element in such stories *(Ackroyd, Moving Finger)* and a suspicion of Black Magic does not go amiss *(The Pale Horse)*. The point to emphasize is that the coziness and the stability are only skin-deep. As John Ritchie observes: "the respectable are the murderers, their victims each other." This being so, the reestablishment of apparent order at the end can never be entirely reassuring, except to the wishful thinker or the superficial reader. Mayhem Parva is a microcosm of the big world, and subject to the same disruptions and disturbances. Or, in Miss Marple's much-quoted words: "human nature is much the same everywhere, and, of course, one has opportunities of observing it at closer quarters in a village" (*Thirteen Problems* [U.S. *The Tuesday Club Murders*], chapter 6). It is in many ways an unrealistic, stylized world: a world, for example, where divorce is mainly an excuse for mystery or melodrama;* where the shifting financial fortunes of the middle-class characters are referred to vaguely, but are seldom *felt* in their everyday living; where something or someone will always turn up to ensure that Miss Marple never has to do her own washing-up. But *cozy,* safe, ordered? Only on the surface.

Is this also an intolerably snobbish world, as critics of the Mayhem Parva school of detective fiction so often allege? Here one must go carefully, and not confuse Agatha Christie with other practitioners. It is instructive to compare her detectives with those of her best-known contemporaries. Christie does not provide us

---

*"Her marriage had recently, as she put it, come unstuck . . ." in the late *Adventure of the Christmas Pudding* is the first example I can find of separation or divorce being accepted as, so to speak, a fact of married life.

with tantalizing hints of noble (or even royal) ancestry, as Margery Allingham and Ngaio Marsh do, still less exhaustive documentation of it, as Dorothy Sayers does.* Her detectives are solidly bourgeois figures. This avoids those exquisitely embarrassing moments so common in her contemporaries when the lady of the manor realizes that the detective, dammit, is a gentleman, and settles into a good natter about genealogies. Christie's documentation of the tastes, prejudices and habits of these bourgeois figures is done with knowledge and sympathy. The class she deals with in these books is simply, as with Jane Austen, the class she knew best. The *Times Literary Supplement* (September 18, 1970) described the English detective story as being "oddly class-bound, emanating from and imbued with the mores of a group one must describe fairly closely as professional middle-middle to upper-middle class." On such matters the *Times* knows best, and we can accept it as a good guide to the social geography of Christie country. Titles are rare in Mayhem Parva, and the highest one is likely to go is a baronet. A peer is a figure not to be trusted:** Lord Edgware has

dark hair streaked with grey, a thin face and a sneering mouth. He looked bad-tempered and bitter. His eyes had a queer secretive look about them. There was something, I thought, distinctly odd about those eyes.

---

*Whether this kind of snobbery is any more ridiculous than the present-day one which has the detective a police superintendent who is also one of the foremost modern poets may be left to the reader to decide.

**Colin Watson in *Snobbery with Violence* contends that "In *Death In The Clouds* [U.S. *Death in the Air*] . . . Mrs Christie had included in the plot a figure traditionally venerated by the public and therefore not to be presented facetiously by any novelist who valued sales—a lord." This is surely nonsense: Christie's treatment of such figures is frequently (in fact almost invariably) tinged with ridicule, satire or suspicion, as was Doyle's (in, for example, "The Noble Bachelor").

In view of the fact that Lord Edgware has a footman who might have posed for a statue of Hermes or Apollo and has on his library shelves both the *Memoirs* of Casanova and books on de Sade and medieval tortures, we can perhaps choose for ourselves the precise nature of the oddness we wish to attribute to him, but this description is all of a piece with Christie's typical country-gentry distrust of the aristocracy. She did not feel at ease with the horse-racing, house-partying, being-presented-at-Court set. In the same book we have a duke with a "weak but obstinate face" who looks like "a weedy young haberdasher," and a duchess straight from not Wilde but the world of children's stories—haughty, rude, accustomed to obedience, surveying the world beneath her through an arrogant lorgnette.

The fact is that Agatha Christie was of the middle-middle class, and had some of the prejudices of the middle-middle class. Most of the characters in her novels are "her sort of people," and the outsider marks himself off clearly as such: the vulgar girl secretary with the cheap silk stockings and the eye for a desirable catch; the private nurse who mingles too freely with her betters and gets unsuitable ambitions; the businessman trying to ape the landed gentry, dismissed by Mrs. Oliver (whom surely we can take as her creator's voice?) as "rich, plebeian and frightfully stupid outside business."

It is not surprising that many modern readers find this sort of thing distasteful. The point that needs to be made, though, is that Agatha Christie does not play on her readers' snobbery in the way many of the "Golden Age" writers did: she did not introduce her readers to a set of characters well above themselves socially, and then invite their complicity in looking downward and sneering.* Margery Allingham's obsessive use of the word *vulgar* is symptomatic here. Nor is her look at her

---

*The "pornography of class" (as he calls it) in Dorothy L. Sayers is very well analyzed by Martin Green in *Transatlantic Patterns.*

own class softened by her presumed sympathy with their views and habits.* As the *Times Literary Supplement* says in the piece just quoted: "She has never been concerned with any of the snobberies indicated above . . . not least because where there is engaged affection, there will be no criminal." Emotional identification with her class would smudge the crystal clearness of the problem and its solution. The tentative law that in an English detective story the least socially acceptable person probably did it does not work at all well with Christie—no more than the statistically to be expected. And if we are invited to sneer or suspect the upstart businessman, we can never be sure that Christie is not playing with our expected responses in order to deceive us: Mrs. Oliver's remark above is taken from *Dead Man's Folly,* and it is as well to read the story through to the denouement before one makes any overeasy accusations of snobbery.

Where the modern reader's distaste for some of the social attitudes in the Christie books seems to me to be more firmly based is in the treatment of servants. Any warm community of feeling between master and servant, the old aristocratic ideal of service and obligation mutually accepted, is quite absent in Christie's fictional world. In life she may have been fond of her own servants and been loved in return (there is evidence that this was so from *An Autobiography* and from those who knew her). But the stance she adopts in the books is very different. Servants in Christie novels of the 'twenties and 'thirties are habitually ridiculed and distrusted. Even a valued old family retainer will be dismissed as having "the characteristics of his class"—a phrase that recurs in the books with monotonous regularity, always carrying strong derogatory overtones. Worst treated of all are those on the lowest level, the house-

*That Christie was also capable of casting a typically cold stare at her own class is suggested by the Mary Westmacott novel *Absent in the Spring,* in which the central character—a managing, middle-class woman, cold, interfering, emotionally undeveloped—is seen very much as a representative of the worst kind of middle-class values. It is an analysis of considerable skill.

maids. They are invariably adenoidal, subnormal or giggly, and boringly repeat that they've always kept themselves respectable and they don't know what mum and dad will say, because they've always kept themselves respectable too. In *The Murder at the Vicarage* alone we have three examples of the female domestic servant: one is the totally incompetent servant at the vicarage, whom the vicar-narrator tries in vain to teach to call him "sir"; another is a cleaning lady to Lawrence Redding, whom he describes as "practically a half-wit, as far as I can make out," though the vicar kindly explains that "That's merely the camouflage of the poor. . . . They take refuge behind a mask of stupidity"; the third is Gladys, kitchen maid at the Old Hall, who is individualized thus:

> . . . he described [her] as more like a shivering rabbit than anything human. Ten minutes were spent trying to put the girl at her ease, the shivering Gladys explaining that she couldn't ever—that she didn't ought, that she didn't think Rose would have given her away, that anyway she had meant no harm, indeed she hadn't. . . .

Examples of this sort of thing could be multiplied ad nauseam, and the odd dignified butler or jolly cook can hardly outweigh the unpleasant impression they make. The female domestic servant was among the most depressed classes of the time, yet Christie has no sympathy with her. It is not that she is treated with amused affection. She is actually treated with contempt.* At any rate nobody would contend that the master-servant relationship in Christie is a cozy one, cozily treated.

There are various lines of defense possible: most of the sneering

---

*One should perhaps emphasize that Christie is not exceptional in this. The novels of Josephine Tey seem to belong to a much more modern world than Christie's, yet as late as 1949 she can perpetrate an enquiry like the following (by the charming and well-born vicar's lady, apropos a new housemaid): "Can your latest moron take a telephone message?" [*Bratt Farrar*] remarks about the servant class are made by characters, and the author could argue that they are only voicing common attitudes of their class. Poirot himself, who feels so superior to the beef-witted English middle-class gentleman, not surprisingly feels even more condescending toward the ill-educated servant. Again, by making her domestics so dim as to be unthinkable as murderers, Christie manages to draw the net more closely around her above-stairs characters. But the real defense is perhaps that the attitude taken toward the domestic-servant class is only a consequence of the cold eye which Christie *as an author* casts on her world as a whole. This has nothing to do with her own personality, which may well have been warm and charming, only with the stance she found it necessary to adopt for her sort of book. "Where there is engaged affection there will be no criminal"—or at any rate the Euclidean progression of problem, investigation and solution will be disturbed. In another sort of book she might have evidenced affection, sympathy, indignation for the lot of the overworked domestic. Here any such emotion would be out of place. Because they were so depressed as a class, only the least promising material went into service. In her experience kitchen maids were ill-educated and inarticulate, so they are made such. Just as country squires are conservative, narrow-minded and strong-willed, and are made such. A detective story is not a romantic novel. Keep emotion well in hand.

John Cawelti maintains in his book *Adventure, Mystery and Romance* that the city is the natural setting for a story of detection. Many of the Sherlock Holmes stories and the continuing saga of crime in California by the "tough" school of American writers would seem to bear him out. But Holmes, in a famous *obiter dicta,* emphatically disagrees:

"It is my belief, Watson, founded upon my experience, that the lowest and vilest alleys in London do not present a more dread-ful record of sin than does the smiling and beautiful countryside. . . . Think of the deeds of hellish cruelty, the hidden wickedness which may go on, year in, year out, in such places, and none the wiser."

Thus, from being essentially urban in the hands of Doyle and his contemporaries, and right up to early Sayers, the English detective story removes, in Christie's hands, to the country, to places which are, to a lesser or greater degree, remote, enclosed, uncomplicated by the disruptions and distractions of the greater world. Here the attention could concentrate itself where, in Christie's view, it truly belonged, on the beautiful, naked simplicity of the problem to be solved.

IV

Surprise! Surprise!

It is difficult to recapture today the sort of outcry that greeted *The Murder of Roger Ackroyd* and its unprecedented and unguessable solution. Arguments raged, friends fell out, and the newspaper columns vied with each other in giving the book gratifying publicity. The air was rent with cries of "foul," "unfair," and "cheat," enunciated with a degree of passion which only a nation of sportsmen can muster. For in 1926 the detective story was the national bingo, the national *Coronation Street,* the national Match of the Day. The older generation of detective-story writers had been displaced by a newer, more 'twenties group, and they were entertainers to the nation. The intelligent man's detective story was but a glint in Dorothy L. Sayers's eye, and way in the future lay the detective story as critique of capitalist society, the detective story as investigator of historical mysteries, the detective story as prober of psychopathic states. Whatever one may feel about the generation of crime writers whom Sir Hugh Greene unfashionably dubs "The Monstrous Regiment of Women," they certainly understood that the detective story was an entertainment, and they went ahead and entertained. The crime novel in 1926 was fun, it was a game with rules—though naturally, as in all the best games, one could argue over the rules. It seems all very remote from today, when the mystery writer is grateful to get five lines in the *Observer,* and has a sneaking suspicion that he hardly deserves even that.

In the great debate over the "fairness" or otherwise of *Ackroyd,* Dorothy L. Sayers defended Christie, and as late as 1951 Christie was still defending herself. It all seems a bit like a comic accused of using smutty material at a Royal Variety Performance. But in the end everyone decided it was all right, that if Agatha had played foul she had invented a new kind of foul the rule book hadn't thought of. And everyone read the book, convinced that *they* would guess it. For one of the most sacred rules of the new game was that the solution could not be revealed, so the newspaper argument, tantalizingly, had to be conducted in a vacuum. But from now on Agatha Christie was confirmed as puller of fast ones to the British nation.

It comes as something of a shock to find from *An Autobiography* that the idea for the *Ackroyd* trick was not her own. It came to her, in fact, in a letter from the then Lord Louis Mountbatten, and she offhandedly remarks that she was ill at the time and she is not sure whether she ever wrote to acknowledge it. One hopes she did. Lord Mountbatten's idea was that the story should be narrated in the first person by someone who at the end of the book is revealed to be the murderer. This idea she combined—the prodigality of youth again! later she would have used the two ideas for two different books—with another from her brother-in-law, who said he would like to see a Watson who turned out to be a criminal. Not wishing to sacrifice Hastings—or perhaps not thinking him bright enough to commit a murder that would deceive Poirot for five minutes—she invented a new sidekick, made him (like Hastings) the narrator of the story, and hey-presto, the trick was done.

Not only was Lord Mountbatten's idea a good one: he showed uncanny insight into who best to send it to, in view of the fact that at the time Christie had only written two full-length detective stories, both fairly orthodox. Perhaps he got the idea from reading *The Man in the Brown Suit*, where part of the story is told in the Master Criminal's diaries. At any rate, it was Agatha Christie, of all the crime writers at the time, who could best use the suggestion, because it is she who habitually triumphs by ingenuity, pure and untrammeled. If he had sent it to Dorothy L. Sayers she would have weighed it down with fine writing and secondary ingenuities. It is the wonderful simplicity of Agatha Christie's deceptions of the reader that keeps the stories of her classic period so fresh and readable. You always want to kick yourself at the end—rather than the author.

And once launched into the "least likely suspect" vein, Agatha Christie never looked back. Perhaps "the least likely suspect" is not the happiest description of the murderers in a Christie story; they might more accurately be described as "the ones never suspected"—the characters in the novel who by one ruse or another the reader has been persuaded not to consider. The former would be a mechanical trick that any reader of average intelligence could be expected to see through after reading one or two Christie books. But he very seldom does, and Raymond Chandler's description of the solution of *Murder on the Orient Express* [U.S. *Murder in the Calais Coach*]—"only a half-wit could guess it"—expresses the exasperation of readers who know they are many times as intelligent as Christie, and yet dammit it's happened again.

The great joy of reading vintage Christie is the knowledge that no holds are barred, that no one is exempt: it is when we forget this that she pulls her most dazzling tricks. I am always outraged, oddly, when I see in bookshops the current British paperback editions of the novels of Patricia Wentworth, with the legend on them: "In the true class and tradition of Agatha Christie"—and not just because this is a blatant trading on the name of a more famous writer. "In the tradition" one could allow: the class area she draws on is invariably country gentryish, her attitudes are basically similar, and her usual detective, Miss Silver, is more or less a copy of Miss Marple. But in the same class? Certainly not. One detail may help to explain my reaction. In Patricia Wentworth we invariably find a pair of young lovers, whose love is in one way or another obstructed until the final chapter. One knows from the beginning that neither of these two will be the murderer: wet though they may be, Patricia Wentworth is involved with them, wishes them well, and will provide them with a well-heeled future. One can never know this with Agatha Christie: her young lovers are never angled to produce warm feelings in the reader. They are pieces on a chessboard, to be calmly considered along with all the other chessmen, their qualities, motives and opportunities weighed coldly.

From time to time during her career, then, Christie brought off a series of outrageous coups that kept alive the reputation she gained with *Ackroyd.* When the time for a solution came round, the most unaccountable rabbits were produced from her hat: the murderer was the investigating policeman, he was a child, he was one whom we had thought already dead, he was all the suspects together, he was Poirot, and so on—the trick, as we have said, being always basically the same, that we have been persuaded to omit that particular possible solution from our calculations. So extreme and all-embracing was her ingenuity that she is the despair of later crime writers: because she dared to think the unthinkable there is no trick in the trickster's book, it seems, that she hasn't thought of first. The only variation the present writer can imagine that she did not use was the basis of Margery Allingham's *Police at the Funeral* (1931), and probably it was never used because she naturally liked to be the originator rather than the copier. Her tricks are of such a translucent simplicity that she can use them a second time and we are still deceived: *Endless Night* is so different in setting and characterization that we do not expect her to pull the narrator-murderer trick again; the cunning reversal which served so beautifully in *Hercule Poirot's Christmas* [U.S. *Murder for Christmas*] is changed a little, polished up, and serves for "Three Blind Mice"—which in the form of *The Mousetrap* has been ambushing the unwary for nearly thirty years.

If Agatha Christie has a delicate sense of what is just on the borderline of "fairness" and stops herself before she strays over into the penalty area, she also has a wonderful understanding of the conventions of the detective-story genre, and how they can be used against the reader. Take for example the solution to *Murder on the Orient Express,* so heartily despised by Raymond Chandler. The convention had grown up (with active nurturing from Christie herself) that in a detective story it was quite likely that one or more of the possible suspects would turn out to be an impostor of one kind or another, and much more closely connected to the dead person than he or she pretends. One accepts this up to a certain point, but not beyond. In *Orient Express* we are made aware that one after another of the passengers is connected with the Armstrong kidnapping case, until, just as we are about to cry "this is absurd! No arm of coincidence could be that long!" up jumps Poirot to say exactly the same: this can't be coincidence, this can only be conspiracy—and all the suspects must have had a hand in the murder. Yet the convention is one that Christie blithely stretches at other times (notably in *A Murder Is Announced* and "Three Blind Mice") without ever feeling obliged to point out to the reader its essential absurdity.

It is perhaps relevant at this point, since we are talking about the murderers themselves, to note that *Orient Express* is, I think, one of only two Christies where the criminals at the end are let off scot free (the other is the play *The Unexpected Guest,* where the murder is in revenge for manslaughter). They had rid the world of a monster the law could not reach, and they are therefore not punished. This is a natural extension of Christie's respect in the thrillers for people who take the law into their own hands—and in its turn it is pushed to its logical conclusion in the solution to *Curtain.* In general Agatha Christie is much more worried in these stories about whether the law will be adequate to punish crime than she is about whether it may err. One of the few Christie opinions which come over strongly from the books is one in favor of capital punishment. "Everything he did was bold and audacious and cruel and greedy," exclaims Miss Marple at the end of *4.50 from Padding-ton* [U.S. *What Mrs. McGillicuddy Saw!*] "and I am really very, very sorry . . . that they have abolished capital punishment because I do feel that if there is anyone who ought to hang, it is Dr. Quimper." We feel the author's firm "Hear, hear" in the background here. It is noticeable how sparingly Christie uses the time-honored device of saving an innocent person from the gallows. When, in *Ordeal by Innocence,* the plot hangs on the fact that someone has died in prison while serving a life sentence for a murder he could not possibly have committed, we find at the end that he was *morally* if not actually responsible. When Poirot or Miss Marple rescues anyone from hanging or life imprisonment (as in *Mrs. McGinty's Dead* and *Nemesis*) they are unsatisfactory, unattractive young men for whom the reader can feel no cheap sympathy, or exaltation at their release. Quite possibly they'll land up in jail again before very long. *Sad Cypress* is the only book where the traditional thrill-jerker is used with all the stops pulled out. On the whole, the books seem to be saying, British justice is the best in the world, and it very rarely makes mistakes.

That we do not err in attributing Miss Marple's (and Poirot's) vigorous approval of the rope to their creator can be seen in *An Autobiography,* where she has a strongly worded passage on the subject:

I am willing to believe that they are made that way, that they are born with a disability, for which, perhaps, one should pity them; but even then, I think, not spare them—because you cannot spare them any more than you could spare the man who staggers out from a plague-stricken village in the Middle Ages to mix with innocent and healthy children in a nearby village.

Perhaps it was her feeling that murderers are dangerous wild beasts, and therefore *must* in some way or another be put out of the way that led her, late in life, to alter the end of "Witness for the Prosecution" from the splendid and tantalizing one in the short story (included in *The Hound of Death*) and the radio-play version to the one in the stage-play and film form—as tawdry a piece of melodrama as ever graced the early Victorian stage: the murderer *had* to be put out of the way, if not by the law then by private revenge. "I wanted that end. I wanted it so much that I wouldn't agree to have the play put on without it," she notes in *An Autobiography* (where elsewhere she claims to have been very easy to persuade). In her vintage years she would not have let a personal opinion override her artistic judgment in this way. In the classic books her feelings about justice and the excellence of British law do not prevent her from using policemen or judges as murderers if it serves her purpose to do so. And the judge's final words in *Ten Little Niggers* [U.S. *And Then There Were None*], one of her most subtle and satisfying conclusions, suggests that she could then understand the moral ambiguities behind law which is not just reformative or preventive, but also retributive:

I was born with other traits besides my romantic fancy. I have a definite sadistic delight in seeing or causing death. I remember experiments with wasps—with various garden pests. . . . From an early age I knew strongly the lust to kill.

But side by side with this went a contradictory trait—a strong sense of justice. It is abhorrent to me that an innocent person or creature should suffer or die by any act of mine. I have always felt strongly that right should prevail.

It may be understood—I think a psychologist would understand—that with my mental make-up being what it was, I adopted the law as a profession. The legal profession satisfied nearly all my instincts.

The surprise at the end of a really good Christie (and *Ten Little Niggers* is a really good Christie) is supremely satisfying to the addict, and yet it is apt to be described by the unhooked as merely a trick, a childish ingenuity beneath serious consideration, one more illustration of the basic silliness of the form. But the revelations in the final chapter of a detective story are no different in kind from, say, the revelation of the meaning of the tests on Gawain and the identity of his tester in the medieval *Sir Gawain and the Green Knight,* or—to take an example remote from popular or folk literature—the revelation (to herself and us) of the true object of Emma Woodhouse's romantic feelings at the end of *Emma.* Both these have the satisfying resolution which comes at the end of all traditional forms involving mystery: in both these cases the reader has struggled to penetrate to the true meaning and significance of strange events, or has been lulled into accepting an interpretation of given facts which is suddenly seen to be precisely contrary to what is now revealed to be the truth. Only the most alert reader of *Emma* will discover the true significance behind the length of time it takes Frank Churchill to fix old Mrs. Bates's spectacles, or Jane Fairfax's embarrassment at the mysterious gift of a piano. The quality of the revelation may be (indeed is) very different to that at the end of a detective story, but the desire to intrigue, mislead, and finally astonish is not beneath Jane Austen, and is basic to many varieties of story telling.

Some of Agatha Christie's solutions, it must be admitted, do not pass the test of satisfying illumination: the way Miss Marple arrives at the identity of the murderer in *4.50 from Paddington* [U.S. *What Mrs. McGillicuddy Saw!*] is never made clear, and might as easily be by divine revelation as by any process of ratiocination. On the other hand, there are the supremely satisfying detective-story solutions (to take a random selection that springs to mind let us name Sayers's *Strong Poison,* Allingham's *Police at the Funeral,* Christie's *Five Little Pigs* [U.S. *Murder in Retrospect*]) where the revelation is felt to be the logical and only possible culmination of what has gone before: it illuminates, explains, has a true feeling of inevitability. If the plotting and placing of clues has been fair, we feel, "It could only have ended like this"—as we do with *Othello, Tom Jones* or *Tess of the D'Urbervilles.*

This sort of satisfaction, the highest, is not, it must be admitted, produced by all, even, of the vintage Christies. It is interesting in this connection to look at her working methods when she was writing a detective story of the classic type. She records in *An Autobiography* that the important time, and the longest—often a matter of many months—was the gestation period. It was then that every detail had to be planned: *why,* when he did this, did she do that? What was the consequence of the revelation of this to the actions of her? The plot, the clues, the strategy of reader-deception were thus planned down to the minutest detail, every move prearranged, every possible objection guarded against. This was the "broody" period. After it came the actual writing of the book— very fast and painless, perhaps only a few weeks.

Very few writers, I suspect, could imagine writing their books after this fashion: most of them, probably, get their best ideas with their pens in their hands; a character only takes on specificity and depth while he is being written about, while his relationships and background are being fleshed out. Most popular writers—and most serious ones too, perhaps—depend on the "happy inspiration," the idea that seems to come unbidden but in fact springs out of the growing solidity which characters, situation and milieu are acquiring as the writing progresses.

Agatha Christie clearly left herself very little room for the happy inspiration, and very little room for the sort of integrated, concrete realization of character that other detective writers (all of them fair and square in the nineteenth-century novel tradition) do effortlessly. There are none of the intense Dickensian grotesques we find in Margery Allingham, none of the thoughtful, realistic studies of moral dilemmas in the George Eliot manner that we find in Josephine Tey. There are few, even, of those quick, vivid character sketches that illumine Lew Archer's grubby pilgrimages through the moral desert of California. This is not said to point to any deficiency in Christie: we must say more about characterization when we come to the speech for the defense. What I am trying to point at here is the different balance in her books, when compared with her contemporaries. When she praised the novels of Margery Allingham because "everything she writes has a definite shape. . . . each book has its own separate and distinctive character" she put her finger on what marked Allingham off from herself. Looking back on Allingham we never remember any particular detective feat of Campion's; we remember atmospheres, milieus: London in a pea-souper, Bloomsbury in decay. Atmospheric background of this sort was not in Christie's line, because it would distract attention from the central business (for her) of the detective story: the puzzle, the sleight-of-hand. The same sort of consideration applied to characterization in depth. Her methods of planning (and her description of the detective story, quoted earlier, as *"technically* interesting" is indicative of her whole approach) left her no room for maneuver: the happy chance in the course of writing could only disturb the beautiful layout of the puzzle. Therefore the characters, with a few exceptions, are penny-plain, cardboard-cut-out figures—though ones that admirably suit the sort of book she aims to write.

For though Poirot frequently brandishes psychology in our faces and exhorts us to use it in solving the crime, we don't need to worry: we are not going to be exposed to the Freudian naïvetés of the American school or the murky in-depth analyses of some recent British practitioners. He means by psychology nothing more than a breezy generalization about how the jealous woman scorned instinctively behaves in a given situation, or what the timid man does in the face of danger—nothing more than the sort of folk wisdom about human behavior one might expect from an advice-to-the-lovelorn column. There is nothing in Poirot's "psychology" that has not been a cliché of the journeyman playwright for the past two or three thousand years. Even in the best Christies the characterization has an *appearance* of solidity rather than genuine depth, and there can be no psychology where there is no depth of characterization.

Thus, one can make some elementary distinctions about the kind and quality of the surprises that Christie springs in the final pages. There are the supreme examples, meticulously planned, in which either the plotting of the incidents or some apparent depth in the characterization gives the revelation of the truth a particularly satisfying quality. *Five Little Pigs* has a solution on this level. Then there are the more average examples, which are simple surprises based on her skill in distracting attention from the obvious by narrative strategy or misleading clueing. In most of these we accept the revelation about the identity of the murderer without too much trouble because none of the characters has been drawn with such depth that we have been convinced of their *in*ability to commit the crime. Examples of this good average Christie thriller might be *Death in the Clouds* [U.S. *Death in the Air*] or *Hercule Poirot's Christmas* [U.S. *Murder for Christmas*]. Most of the vintage Christie work is on this level, in fact: we are delighted with the surprise because it is borne in on us *how* she has been fooling us throughout the story. This is the same kind of emotion we feel when we look up the answer to yesterday's four across in the *Times* crossword, and begin to unwind the tangle of the clue which defeated us.

And then, on the lowest level, there are solutions which fail to satisfy us, and it is interesting to analyze *why* we feel cheated or disappointed at the end of some of the stories. For the most part the trouble lies in what we are required to believe: the detective writer treads a delicate path between bare credibility and sheer incredibility, and it is perilously easy to stray over the border. It might be worthwhile looking at a couple of solutions which fail to satisfy, and trying to see why.

The Murder at the Vicarage is one of those stories where the most likely suspect is proved conclusively at the beginning to have been unable to commit the murder and proved conclusively at the end to have done so. This was the initial impetus behind *The Mysterious Affair at Styles,* and since the perpetration of this murder also depends on collusion it is in type rather close to it, and to *Death on the Nile* and *Evil under the Sun.* The plan, however, does not only depend on collusion; it depends on Miss Marple being in her garden at a certain time of day, on her noticing that Mrs. Protheroe has on her body no conceivable place where a weapon might be concealed, and on a number of other circumstances which may be likelihoods but cannot in the nature of things be certainties. The reader rebels—nobody in their senses would *plan* a murder in that way. Murders in real life may often be puzzling by chance, by a lucky (or unlucky, depending on viewpoint) falling out of things, but murders in detective stories are always deeply laid plans, and the idea of anyone concocting a plan with so many imponderables and incalculables makes the reader dig in his heels and say, "Ridiculous!" Similar objections may be raised against the solution of *Murder in Mesopotamia,* though here they are based partly on characterization. Even if this is sketchy, we want a real attempt made to convince us that the man who throughout the book has been depicted as a besottedly devoted husband has in fact been planning to kill his wife for months because of her suppressed and unconsummated affair with another member of his dig. And we are certainly not happy when we are required to believe that this long-meditated plan depends on the victim putting her head out of her window when a painted mask is tapped against the windowpane, that the murderer could bank on nobody visiting her room for an hour after she was killed to establish his alibi, that she can have been married twice to the same man without realizing the fact, that. . . .

No—the detective story reader can believe six impossible things before breakfast, but to imagine a murderer whose plot depended on so many imponderables—well, as Chandler said: "A murderer who needs that much help from Providence must be in the wrong business."

V

The Disappearing Author

It seems to be inevitable that a great deal will be written in the near future about the sensational disappearance of Agatha Christie in December 1926. At the end we shall no doubt be wiser as to some of the disputed details, but whether we shall be closer to certainty about the essentials of the matter—her state of mind, her motivation—is open to doubt. Like Dickens, Agatha Christie left behind her one last unsolved and unsolvable mystery.

The ingredients of the affair are not unlike those of several of her books. There is the husband, Colonel Archie Christie—charming, brave, attractive and (one guesses) totally selfish and amoral. He is treated sympathetically throughout *An Autobiography,* and yet the impression is conveyed of a creature utterly careless of the feelings of others, mindlessly devoted to his own trivial pleasures and well-being. Whether this double-image of him is the result of artlessness or art on Agatha Christie's part I find it impossible to decide.

Then there is the other woman, secretary to a business friend, with whom Archie Christie began the affair during the summer months of 1926, while Agatha was clearing up the family home and affairs after the death of her mother. By December the affair had progressed so far that she (the secretary) and Archie Christie were weekending together at a friend's house, though he was still living with Agatha at their recently acquired house, The Styles.

Lastly there is Agatha, the injured wife, inevitably the most painful part in all such triangles. On the morning of December 6 she and Archie had (according to press reports) a violent quarrel. In the evening she drove from home, and later her car was found overturned and abandoned in a chalk pit on the Surrey Downs. There was no sign whatsoever of the owner.

At first everything seemed to point to murder, and not surprisingly the police (there were in fact *two* police forces involved in the case, those of Berkshire and Surrey, working against each other in comic detective story fashion) focused their attention on Colonel Christie as the obvious murderer. Several hundred police combed the area for clues or a body, as did a yelping pack of Fleet Street reporters and literally thousands of members of the general public, delighted to take part in a real-life detective story. After ten days Mrs. Christie was found, after a tip-off to a newspaper, at a Harrogate hotel, where she had been staying throughout the time of the uproar. She had registered in the name of the woman with whom Colonel Christie was having an affair. She had lived perfectly openly, joined in the social life of the hotel, charmed the other guests. When challenged by reporters from the *Daily News* she claimed to be suffering from amnesia.

These are the bare facts. The conduct and morals of the other two sides of the triangle need not concern us, but there will always be speculation about Agatha Christie's part in the affair. The press of the time took it as a publicity stunt. This seems quite incredible, not just because *Roger Ackroyd* was already the sensation of the day and had no need of such spectacular boosting, but also because it is totally out of character: a rather conventional, well-brought-up, middle-class young lady might bring herself to indulge in a publicity stunt, but surely not one based on the painful breakup of her own marriage.

Then there is the intriguing possibility that the disappearance was "staged" by a woman of undoubtedly ingenious mind as a piece of revenge on the man who had humiliated her. This was certainly how it worked out: the police acted almost throughout on the assumption (painfully *obvious* to the detective-story addict) that the husband was the most likely murderer. Archie Christie, pushed into a corner, went to the ungentlemanly lengths of telling reporters that his wife had claimed to him that "she could disappear at will," thus pointing the way directly to the assumption that the whole thing was a publicity stunt. But it availed him little all the time she was undiscovered, and someone who had told his wife "I'm no good, remember, if things go wrong . . . I don't like ill people, and I can't bear people to be unhappy or upset" must assuredly have had the most painful and embarrassing ten days of his life. And yet—the same objections apply: to revenge herself on Archie, Agatha Christie focused nationwide attention on the breakup of her own marriage, her own humiliation (which she seems to have felt acutely) as discarded wife. It does not add up.

There remains the possibility that she was suffering from amnesia, or some other form of mental disturbance. Lord Ritchie Calder, in an article written after her death, dismissed the idea of a publicity stunt, but he also discounted entirely the possibility of amnesia. He has a special claim to be heard on the matter, as he was one of the two reporters who "found" her and first talked to her in the Harrogate hotel: "She answered to 'Mrs Christie' and when asked how she got there she said that she did not know and was suffering from amnesia. . . . 'Amnesia' was much too clinical a word for someone surprised into conversation." He does concede, rather reluctantly, that there might have been some other kind of mental disturbance, though it is clear from Gwen Robyns's *The Mystery of*

Agatha Christie that he believes the second explanation above.

Agatha Christie, in *An Autobiography,* says nothing whatsoever about the disappearance, though references in later sections of the book to the horrible newspaper publicity she had received suggest that she may have intended to say something, if she could bring herself to do so. The fact that she mentions her "revulsion against the Press," and that she and her secretary/friend Carlo divided her acquaintances into "Faithful Dogs" and "Rats" (the latter people "anxious to disassociate themselves from anybody who had attracted notoriety of the wrong sort") suggests strong and generalized feelings of bitterness about her treatment after the affair. Even more interesting, though, in connection with the disappearance, is the account she gives of her state of mind earlier in that same year. When her mother died she had gone to Ashfield, her old home near Torquay, to go through the mountains of accumulated family possessions. Archie, as always avoiding illness or unhappiness of any kind, was in London—apparently beginning the affair which was to end the marriage, and refusing even to visit her. In a mood of mounting unhappiness and loneliness Agatha Christie went through with the work, but she records several signs of dubious mental balance: for instance, she is about to sign a check, and cannot remember her own name; she racks her brain, but all she can think of is the name of a character from Thackeray—Blanche Amory, the sexually unscrupulous woman in *Pendennis.* (The similarity of this incident to the signing of her husband's mistress's name in the Harrogate hotel register suggests that *An Autobiography* is misleading here, that the affair antedated Agatha's period in Torquay, or that she was at least suspicious on the subject before she left.)

In the circumstances, and for what it is worth, I would unhesitatingly plump for amnesia or some other extreme mental disturbance. Lord Ritchie Calder's confident pronouncements about the manifestations of this or that type of mental trouble do not ring true to experience. One's only reservation would be that the account of her mental state earlier in the year is Agatha's alone, and she is, after all, mistress of the misleading clue. But what is important here is the effect on her, as a person and a writer, of all the weeks of notoriety and of the intense public scrutiny of her private life. "I had felt like a fox, hunted, my earths dug up and yelping hounds following me everywhere," she wrote in the *Autobiography*. From that time on she was an obsessively private person, unwilling to give even the most innocuous kind of interview or make public appearances. She built herself a thick wall of privacy, with few but her immediate family on the inside.

This refusal to give herself away publicly, this guarding from scrutiny of her deeper feelings, is one of her great strengths as a writer, in particular the source of her success as a constructor of detective-story plots. In her classic phase she is icily detached from her characters, the places they live in, and from any opinion or attitude they may hold. Patricia Wentworth loves her young lovers and could never allow them to be either victims or murderers. Dorothy L. Sayers is besotted with Lord Peter. Agatha Christie feels no emotions toward any of her creations: perhaps Poirot rouses a flicker of irritation, Miss Marple a flicker of affection, but that is all one could say. Each of her characters is surveyed, analyzed, dissected as murderer-potential, without an ounce of involvement. She may now and then get into their minds, describe their feelings, but the reader is not encouraged to feel any emotional identification during this process. He analyzes the thoughts, for clues, for vital omissions. Who knows, after *Roger Ackroyd,* if this isn't Agatha bent on fooling us again? And it is because the noninvolvement is total that the puzzle remains paramount, stands at the center of the reader's interest in the book, hard and crystal-clear.

My contention, then, is that an innate shyness in Christie became, after the disappearance, a strong need to withdraw, hide herself, cover her tracks, and that this determination to give away nothing of herself is the secret of her success as a puzzle-maker.

Not only is there no sense of her own personality in the books; she is equally elusive as to her own tastes and opinions. In fact, she sometimes lets us *presume* these, purposely to mislead us. Take, for example, the little remark I quoted in chapter I from Poirot, to the girl who is pursued by two suitors, one charming and unreliable, one steady and dull: "Moral worth is not romantic. It is appreciated however by widows." It comes from *The Mystery of the Blue Train,* the book she wrote during and after her marital troubles and divorce. Here is Agatha warning us, from bitter experience, against the charming rotter and favoring steady worth, the reader is encouraged to say (and the reader in 1929 knew a great deal, or thought he did, about Agatha Christie's private affairs). But it is the dull, worthy young man who turns out to be the murderer, and the ne'er-do-well who gets the girl in the end.

Precisely similar things happen when we look at Christie's social and political attitudes. Most of her xenophobic remarks were in the very early thrillers. In spite of the obvious fact that a character's opinions are not necessarily those of the author, it seems legitimate to assume they are within hailing distance when they are voiced by the delightful heroine or hero, or the sturdy upholder of law and order and Civilization as We Know It. At this stage, and in the thriller mode, Christie was comparatively free of personal inhibitions, and could give herself away. But if we look at a much later, vintage Christie, *One, Two, Buckle My Shoe* [U.S. *The Patriotic Murders*], a much more interesting pattern emerges. This is one of the novels where the apparent intended victim turns out to be the initiator of the murder plot, and one in which the murder is connected (or, rather, is assumed to be for much of the book's length) with a larger, international conspiracy. It was written in the late 'thirties (published 1940), and is rare in that it contains references to current events. There is a mention of King Leopold of the Belgians ("Very fine man . . . so I've always heard"—a reference Christie may well have regretted not long after publication). There is also an obvious allusion to Mosley's fascist organization in a movement called here the "Imperial Shirts." We also have one of Mrs. Christie's unintentionally funny left-wing agitators:

"There's got to be a new deal—the old corrupt system of finance has got to go—this cursed net of bankers all over the world like a spider's web. They've got to be swept away. . . . There's no room in the world today for men like Blunt—men who hark back to the past—men who want to live as their fathers lived or even their grandfathers lived! You've got a lot of them here in England—crusted old diehards—useless worn-out symbols of a decayed era. And, my God, they've got to go. There's got to be a new world. Do you get me—a new world, see?"

To which balderdash Poirot replies: "I see, Mr Raikes, that you are an idealist."

At the center of the book is the figure of Alistair Blunt. He is a conservative banker who apparently stands behind and is the principal prop of the government of Britain: a safe, steady, conventional figure—a financial Stanley Baldwin. Everything in the novel is directed toward building him up as a man after the average middle-class reader's political heart:

"Blunt [says one of the characters, an ex-secret-service man, and therefore allied with Poirot and the forces of law and order] is the kind of man who in private life would always pay his bills and live within his income—whether he'd got twopence a year or several million makes no difference. He is that type of fellow. And he just simply thinks that there's no reason why a *country* shouldn't do the same! No costly experiments. No frenzied expenditure on possible Utopias."

One can feel Hercule Poirot's petty-bourgeois soul sighing, "How right! How sensible!" In fact, later in the book he says to Blunt,

"You stand for all the things that to my mind are important. For sanity and balance and stability and honest dealing."

But that is just before he has Blunt arrested for murder. As John Cawelti (who has a splendid, long analysis of this book in *Adventure, Mystery and Romance*) puts it: "Christie makes the deeper emotional structure of the classical formula, with its emphasis on the restoration of order, function as a means of distracting the reader's attention from the true culprit." And not only has she fooled the reader—she has covered her tracks as well. The reader has been encouraged in his natural desire to commit himself to Alistair Blunt: he has dug his own trap, and fallen into it. And when he finds he has been misled, no opinion one way or the other, on politics or international finance, can be attributed to Agatha Christie. What other mystery writer is so magnificently unpindownable? Think of Josephine Tey on Scottish Nationalism in *The Singing Sands*. Think of Dorothy L. Sayers on everything under the sun.

A similar process to that noted above can be seen at work in the nonpolitical sphere even as late as 1964, when her defensiveness was generally much weaker than formerly. In *At Bertram's Hotel* we are introduced (Allingham fashion) to one of the "many quiet pockets, unknown to all but taxi-drivers" of London's West End, and to Bertram's Hotel, a place where time seems to have stood still, and where one can (in Waugh's phrase about a very different sort of hotel) "draw up great draughts of Edwardian certainty." Here there are lavish breakfasts with infinitely various side dishes, here there is afternoon tea with real muffins and seed cake and other delicacies that disappeared from everyday upper-class life with the war, here there are superb head waiters and countrified chambermaids to minister to every want of the old-school English country gentry. The reader is immediately tempted into an emotional investment in the place: here is Agatha Christie, very old, luxuriating in a unique survival from a way of life long gone, indulging in pure, affectionate nostalgia (which heaven knows she did often enough in her last books). It passes the reader by (though it shouldn't) that what is being insisted upon is the unreality of the place—that it is a façade, a front. So he remains several moves behind Agatha right up to the moment when Miss Marple says:

"It seemed wonderful at first—unchanged you know—like stepping back into the past—to the part of the past that one had loved and enjoyed. . . . But of course it wasn't really like that. I learned (what I suppose I really knew already) that one can never go back, that one should not even try to go back. . . ."

The reader's assumption that he is experiencing an elderly woman's rambling exercise in nostalgia is turned against him, and Bertram is exposed as an elaborate fraud.

Similar things happen in *Endless Night* (1967) in the introduction of the central character—and the ventriloquism of these first sections, where she catches marvelously the style, attitudes, staccato utterances of the young and classless is far and away the best thing she did in her last years. The reader well read in his Christie (and perhaps having been caught out by *One, Two* [U.S. *The Patriotic Murders*]) will by now have registered her dislike of "safety first," of too much security and self-insurance, and they will recognize the attitude in the protest of the young man who narrates the story:

They wanted me to go steady with a nice girl, save money, get married to her and then settle down to a nice steady job. Day after day, year after year, world without end, amen. Not for yours truly! There must be something better than that. Not just all this tame security, the good old welfare state limping along in its half-baked way! Surely, I thought, in a world where man has been able to put satellites in the sky and where men talk big about visiting the stars, there must be *something* that rouses you, that makes your heart beat, that's worth while searching all over the world to find!

The reader warms to this narrator. And forgets that if there is one thing that an experienced Christie reader ought to beware of, it is warming to narrators.

All these examples show Christie allowing the reader to *assume* an attitude (to life, society, politics, morality) on her part, and then turning it against the reader when it comes to the solution. D. H. Lawrence said that as soon as you try to pin anything down in the novel, either you kill the novel or the novel gets up and walks away with the nail. One might say that as soon as the reader tries to nail anything down in Agatha Christie, the author ups and stabs him with the pin. It is this compulsive hiding of personality and opinions, this obsessive reticence, that is Agatha Christie's greatest strength as a public deceiver.

This emotional detachment might seem, at first sight, to disable Agatha Christie as a popular writer; is it not the arousing of easy, cheap emotion that is the very core of success in mass fiction? Well —often, but not always. Part of the success of the Sherlock Holmes stories lies in the glacial emotional detachment Conan Doyle manages to maintain—both from the crimes and their victims, and also from his famous duo: the pathetic joy with which Watson greets any scrap of gratitude or affection Holmes deigns to throw in his direction only serves to highlight the prevailing chill over Baker Street. In "The Dancing Men" Holmes even allows his client to be killed, without displaying undue emotion. In a very different way the same is true of that human machine James Bond. In the case of all three authors the weight of the story is in the plot elements—suspense, action, surprise. In addition, all three manage to chime in with one of the dominant moods of the twentieth century: a distrust of personal feeling, an emotional cynicism, a distaste for involvement.

There is one other rather odd consequence of Christie's desire to make herself as anonymous as possible, to disappear from her own books. It would be quite impossible, in the books of the classic period, to hazard any guess at the author's tastes—for example, in music, literature, architecture or whatever. We know she was fond of music: she had studied in Paris, considered the possibility of a professional career, loved opera, and had a grand piano always near her for her own use. When the anthology of articles was assembled which paid tribute to her after her death *(Agatha Christie, First Lady of Crime)* it must have seemed a good idea to have one on music in the novels. William Weaver, a first-rate critic of both music and detective fiction, undertook the task—but it must sorely have taxed even his abilities. He could make nothing of his subject, because there was nothing to make anything from. Not only are the musical references few: what there are, are as conventional, blank and anonymous as her settings. Nothing more individual than a few passing references to Mendelssohn's "Songs without Words", or the "Dead March" from *Saul.* The same could be said of the references to literature. We know from elsewhere that Christie was decidedly well read in an idiosyncratic, self-educated way. We find references to *Peer Gynt,* to the late T. S. Eliot, as well as a deep knowledge of Shakespeare, Dickens and the major Victorian novelists. But in the detective stories? Well, there are the nursery rhymes, of course, but beyond them the quotes are, again, of the most tired and threadbare: "Who would have thought the old man to have had so much blood in him?"; "The mills of God grind slow . . ."; "God's in his heaven, All's right with the world." The luxury of a reference to *Our Mutual Friend* (not well-known Dickens at the time, though a mine of quotation for other detective-story writers of the Golden Age) occurs in *Styles,* but would be unlikely in the classic period. To be sure, there are some more recondite quotations buried in the text from time to time, but only a well-read reader could spot them. Even one's choice of quotation, she seems to have felt, could give one away. Once again, she refuses to stamp her books with any individuality, if by that is meant the individuality of one's own tastes and interests.

That famous, overdiscussed disappearance of 1926 was, then, a prelude to a figurative disappearance of the author, one that involved the suppression of all traits and tastes and idiosyncrasies from her own works. The author was an irrelevance—just as she felt that a love interest in detective stories was an irrelevance to "what should be a scientific process." There are many readers who think they have pinned her down, who sneer at her, often, for what they think they have diagnosed about her, but what has happened, usually, is that they have been caught out by one of Christie's many strategies of deception.

VI

Strategies of Deception

In the course of her more than five decades as a professional and prolific writer of detective fiction Agatha Christie acquired for her armory a variety of "strategies of deception," means of deceiving the reader which she experimented with, developed and perfected over the years. The phenomenon noticed in the last chapter—her withdrawal of herself from her own books, the way she hides her personality, tastes and attitudes and invites the reader to *assume* things about her opinions as a way of tricking him—is one of those strategies, and one of the most elusive and difficult to guard against. There are others that the attentive reader may more confidently feel he has identified and can ensure himself against, though more often than not he finds that Christie has invented some minor variation of the trick, or some extra twist in the tangled skein, and that once again he has been caught on the hop.

The most popular of these strategies, which turns up time and time again in various forms, is a development of the *Roger Ackroyd* trick, though this one depends not so much on point of view as on point of sympathy. In *Roger Ackroyd* we exclude a character from our suspicions because we see the action through his eyes; in this strategy we exclude him because we are placed in a position of sympathy with him from the beginning. What we have here is not a pattern of narrator as murderer, but one of assumed victim as murderer, or pursuer as murderer. In these books the *donnée* of the story is the pursuit of an unidentified criminal by someone who seems to be the object of a series of murder attempts *(Peril at End House),* who seems to be the victim of some sort of conspiracy *(One, Two, Buckle My Shoe* [U.S. *The Patriotic Murders*] and *By the Pricking of My Thumbs,* for example), or who is sure there has been committed an undetected murder *(Three Act Tragedy* [U.S. *Murder in Three Acts*]). It is at the beginning of a book (when he is merely "getting into the story," collecting the necessary data) that the reader is least wary: because the whole investigation starts off from this *donnée* the initiator is exempt from suspicion, he is allied with Poirot or whomever in the search for truth. We are fooled because Christie has worked her favorite piece of legerdemain—she has persuaded us right from the beginning to see the situation the wrong way up.

It is not, of course, a trick peculiar to Agatha Christie. The initiator of the chase who turns out to be the guilty party occurs now and then in Conan Doyle, for example in "The Adventure of the Priory School." It is a trick that Ross Macdonald pulls so often, with Lew Archer apprehending at the end of the book the man who engaged him at the beginning, that one has the gravest doubts about the financial viability of the Archer detective agency. This particular deception works best with the sort of elbow room that the *novel* gives: when Christie tries it (several times) in the short stories that make up *Poirot Investigates* it is ineffective because the restricted length does not permit any real reader-identification with the supposed victim or pursuer. On the other hand the initiators of the pursuit in *Peril at End House, Three Act Tragedy, Endless Night* and *A Murder Is Announced* are significantly superior to the norm in Christie characterization: either they are marked by strongly individual personalities or else they engage the sympathy of the reader by the pathos and interest of their situation, and thus he is happy to associate them with the principal sleuth in the crusade for truth and justice. When the solution comes around, however, the reader is reminded how frequently the negative potentialities of these characters have been placed before him.

This particular strategy is allied to another favorite one whereby the actual investigator (*Curtain,* "Three Blind Mice") or the sidekick Watson figure as recommended by Agatha Christie's brother-in-law *(Hercule Poirot's Christmas* [U.S. *Murder for Christmas*], *They Came to Baghdad)* is finally unmasked as the villain. What Christie relies on here, of course, is the familiar tendency of the British detective story (as opposed to the American) to give unequivocal support to the established forces of law and order. The police may be ridiculed, but their essential honesty of intention can generally be taken for granted, outside Christie.

In this strategy Christie deceives the reader by using the traditional attitudes inherent in the detective-story convention, but she also harks back, probably quite consciously, to the very origins of crime fiction. Jerry Palmer (in *Thrillers,* pp. 180 et seq.) draws attention to the well-known ambiguity in the popular attitude to crime, its unpredictable tendency to elevate the criminal to heroic status and anathematize his pursuer. Inevitably this blurring around the moral edges finds its way into writings about crime in the eighteenth and early nineteenth centuries. The ethical uncertainties inherent in the pursuit of a criminal were at the heart of William Godwin's *Caleb Williams,* so much so that guilt and innocence are most uncertainly distributed between pursuer and pursued. In fact, skepticism about the forces of law goes back much further, at least to the figure of Jonathan Wild who so fascinated Fielding and later Harrison Ainsworth (the latter's *Jack Shepherd* in which Wild figures prominently involves attitudes to crime and social conformity which are a mess of unassimilated contradictory impulses). The mixed emotions the young Dickens felt on the subject of the criminal and his apprehension is easily illustrated by the chapters in *Oliver Twist* describing the pursuit and death of Bill Sikes. Here the crowd representing the lawful indignation of the community is depicted as a sort of lynch mob, with Mr. Brownlow as its unlikely leader. The reader is excited, disturbed, appalled, but undoubtedly *with* Sikes rather than Brownlow. In *Bleak House* (Agatha Christie's favorite Dickens) the French maid Hortense is both pursuer of Lady Dedlock and the real perpetrator of the murder she is suspected of, and this pattern was clearly important to Dickens because at the end of his life he was engaged with a similarly ambiguous figure, John Jasper, who (we must assume, since *Edwin Drood* remained unfinished) was the murderer or intended the murder of his nephew and at the same time the one "dedicated to the destruction" of his slayer. In other words, Christie was taking an attitude already well established in crime literature, and adapting it to the particular needs of the puzzle-type detective story.

Many of Christie's other strategies of deception also involve the use and twisting of well-worn literary material, of cliché situations and stereotyped characters from popular fiction, where she can predict the reader's response and use it against him. One such strategy, very well analyzed by Emma Lathen in *Agatha Christie, First Lady of Crime,* uses that perennial literary standby, the eternal triangle. In its most usual form in Christie we are likely to be presented as a starting point with a marriage that is threatened from outside by an alluring and sexually unscrupulous type, usually a woman. The husband is attracted, and the reader's sympathy is inevitably drawn toward the innocent party (the wife) and away from the husband and the marriage-breaker. There is of course a special interest in the recurrence of this pattern because of its relevance to the breakup of Agatha Christie's own marriage. Yet, true to her habits of self-concealment, any easy sympathy the reader may feel for the injured wife almost always turns out to be a snare, and the pattern never remains in its pristine, morally unambiguous shape. The triangle is the basis of at least three of the novels of the classic period (*Death on the Nile, Evil under the Sun* and *Five Little Pigs* [U.S. *Murder in Retrospect*]) and several short stories, most notably "Triangle at Rhodes" and "The Bloodstained Pavement." In every case Christie relies on a standardized literary situation, and she pulls off her deception because we can see no further than the cliché. In the denouement to the plot we tend to find that it is the marriage, or the earliest love relationship, that is the enduring one (in either a positive or a negative way), and that it is the intruder who is deceived, to be pitied, and frequently the victim. Notice how *Death on the Nile* and *Evil under the Sun* have virtually identical plots: the stable initial relationships (Simon Doyle–Jacqueline de Belfort in the one, the Redfern marriage in the other) are apparently threatened by a desirable outsider (Linnet Ridgeway with her money, Arlena Marshall with her looks). In both cases the murder is a conspiracy of the original couple against the outsider.*

In these stories the triangle is an open one, clear from the beginning; in other books the same material is used but the triangle is concealed, certain basic information being withheld from the reader. Significantly these tend to be late books, for toward the end of her life Christie became less concerned with the 'twenties imperative of playing fair. Thus, in *A Caribbean Mystery* the liason between Tim Kendal and Esther Walters is kept from us, and so in *Endless Night* is that between the narrator and Greta. But it was obviously a pattern that fascinated Christie, and the interested reader can trace the way she worked out all sorts of variations on it in such novels as *Elephants Can Remember, Towards Zero,* and *Sad Cypress.*

---

*Note Christie's frequent use of conspiracies between two suspects who are individually "impossible" murderers and apparently unlikely partners.

It was not only when she was dealing with the eternal triangle that Christie showed her skill in taking formulas from popular literature (which after all was what she was writing, with the difference that she was out to deceive) where she could rely on a certain response to certain stimuli, and using that response as a way of leading the reader up an enticingly familiar garden path. We have seen that skill at work already in *One, Two, Buckle My Shoe* [U.S. *The Patriotic Murders*]: faced with the setup of an international conspiracy to murder a conservative banker on whom the stability of Britain depends, the reader reacts in a predictable way which ensures he averts his eyes from the suspiciousness of the banker himself. There are plenty of other examples: faced in *Endless Night* with the poor-boy-marries-heiress formula, done from the point of view of the poor boy, with emphasis laid on the hostility and greed of the heiress's relatives, the reader forgets the suspicions of the boy's intentions he would certainly feel in real life; faced in *Death on the Nile* with an heiress who uses her money unscrupulously to assert her power, and who apparently steals her best friend's fiancé, the reader lets his sympathies go out unreservedly to the best friend; faced in *Murder in Mesopotamia* with a bitch wife and a complaisant, besotted husband, the reader forgets that in real life the most likely killer of a wife is a husband. In all these cases the familiar garden path is transformed by the conclusion of the story into a bewilderingly strange emotional landscape.

In characterization, too, Christie often creates a pure stereotype, hoping that the reader will discount a figure so obviously drawn from stock—a piece from her standard repertory of cardboard figures, and given one of her standard names (Caroline for elderly inquisitive spinsters, prissy trisyllabic names for lawyers, and so on). One such piece of cardboard is Major Burnaby in *The Sittaford Mystery* [U.S. *Murder at Hazelmoor*]—bluff, down-to-earth, a bit of a bore in men's company, a bit uneasy in women's. We discount him, partly because we have seen so many other such figures on the outskirts of Christie stories, partly because the discovery of the body is apparently done from his point of view (though actually Christie keeps well away from his thoughts at this moment, and uses an *Ackroyd* trick, ignoring his activities for a significant length of time). Similarly Christie banks on a certain reader-response to other stock characters—American lady-tourists are merely funny, children are innocent, old ladies are frail and nice—in every case the stock response being used as a means of diverting suspicion from where suspicion is due.

One of the main weapons in Christie's armory of deception is her supreme skill in diverting the reader's attention from the matter of real importance by focusing his attention on some irrelevancy elsewhere. The words "conjuring trick" occur over and over again in reviews of her books, and this is of course the essence of the conjuror's art. This skill is of great importance when clues are being placed, as we shall see, but it can also be seen at work in major matters of plotting as well. For example, there are many books in which the reader is sent off after a false scent by being persuaded to give his attention to the wrong murder, or to an attempted murder that is in reality no more than a smoke screen. Like the pursuer-murderer trick, with which it is often allied, this usually relies on a *donnée* for a novel which is finally seen to be a highly deceptive piece of conjuror's art.

This ploy has been seen in several of the books we have already looked at, most notably *Peril at End House* and *One, Two, Buckle My Shoe*. There are many more: in *Three Act Tragedy* [U.S. *Murder in Three Acts*] we have our attention focused on the murder of the Reverend Stephen Babbington; in *A Murder Is Announced* on the theatrically set up "shooting" of Lettie Blacklock; in *By the Pricking of My Thumbs* on the supposed threat to the aged Mrs. Lancaster. These are the starting points of the stories. Only they turn out to be the wrong starting points. This technique is seen at its most elaborate in *The ABC Murders* (which is the "real" murder, which are part of the smokescreen?), and at its most beguiling in *After the Funeral* [U.S. *Funerals Are Fatal*]. Here the story is set on its way by the tactless remark at the funeral of Richard Abernethy: "But he *was* murdered, wasn't he?" and by the death immediately afterward of Cora Lansquenet, the person who said it. This establishes in the reader's mind a cause-and-effect sequence, with the *initial* death —Abernethy's—as apparently the more important one. Whereas in fact Richard Abernethy is one of the few people in any of Christie's novels to die from natural causes, and the important death is in fact that of Cora Lansquenet.

In analyzing the use of these and all the rest of her stratagems of deception, the question is bound to arise of Agatha Christie's relationship with her reader—always a ticklish problem, as witness the case of Dorothy L. Sayers, whose rather superior manner and aggressively conservative stance chimed in perfectly with her readers' demands in the 'twenties and 'thirties but tend to put readers off today. It would certainly have been easy for Agatha Christie to alienate her audience by the relentless trickiness of her mind. But this never seems to happen, and it may be that her popularity so far outstrips that of her rivals—better writers, more vivid characterizers, nearly as ingenious plotters—because she creates an entirely satisfactory relationship, based on what one might call trustful mistrust. This is attested to by the frequency with which one hears her readers say that she "always plays fair." Where the plots of her competitors depended on detailed knowledge of railway timetables, minutiae of forensic science, a grasp of engineering that could invent yet more fantastic ways of killing men in a locked room—in a word, specialist knowledge of one kind or another—she demanded from her reader only a noticing eye and ear, and a lively grasp of the facts of everyday life around him. Though one has doubts about the use of the word *cozy* to describe her books, certainly it is true to say that the means she uses to unmask her villains are "homely" in the English sense— that is, they are commonplace things one meets with every day. In *Death in the Clouds* [U.S. *Death in the Air*] she plays around satirically with darts tipped with the poison of the South American

Indians, but the real clues are things like an empty matchbox, an extra coffeespoon in a saucer. Thus, though her stories are intellectual puzzles of a certain rarefied kind, she manages to "earth" them by her constant use of commonplace objects from the life around us. The reader feels that the clues relate to his experience, and therefore *ought* to tell him the truth: he blames his own imperceptiveness when the time for the solution comes round, not the author for a showy display of esoteric knowledge.

Julian Symons tells a good story in this connection. He was to attend a Detection Club dinner, but, arriving late, he slipped straight into his chair just as everyone else was finishing their soup. He found that, at the bottom of the table, he was facing Agatha Christie in the place of honor at the top, and that, unnervingly, her eyes were fixed upon him. Was it reproof for lateness? Was he improperly dressed? Then he realized that her eyes were fixed on his hands, and that they were dirty. Her mind was playing around with the possibilities of a man, impeccably dressed for a formal occasion, but with dirty hands. Sherlock Holmes says that the world is full of obvious things which nobody by any chance ever observes. It is this that Agatha Christie, like Doyle, capitalized upon. One has the impression that, always, she went around looking for things—ordinary, domestic, trivial things—from which something deceptive could be made. She kept a desk full of clues—everyday things that she had thought of a use for. Even poison, which she loved using because she had a special knowledge of it, is the most domestic mode of murder. Shooting, which requires a special knowledge of guns which neither she nor her average reader possessed, very seldom figures in her books. She also had a wonderful memory for sinister oddities from her actual experience. Her boss in the dispensary in the First World War kept a lump of curare in his pocket: "Do you know why?" he asked her. "It gives me a sense of power." She used this in a book, but one written *fifty years* later.

And her *placing* of these clues is miraculously sure, again ensuring that warm readership trust which built her up a devoted following which (unlike Sayers's) still seems strong in the younger generation today. There was the vital piece of information placed before us, we tend to say at the end of a Christie, but we ignored it because of the *way* it was placed. One much-quoted example is the butler and the calendar in *Hercule Poirot's Christmas.* An even better example, because it illustrates how well Christie understood the working of her readers' minds, occurs in *The Sittaford Mystery* [U.S. *Murder at Hazelmoor*]. The opening chapters, up to the discovery of Captain Trevelyan's body, occur on the fringes of a Dartmoor deep in snow, with a new blizzard threatening (one of very few examples in Christie of a precise geographical placing). In the first chapter we are told that Major Burnaby and Captain Trevelyan used to go to Switzerland together for the winter sports. Shortly after the finding of the body we are told that there are two pairs of skis in the cupboard of Captain Trevelyan's dining room. But Christie knows her readers: to the English—particularly at the time she wrote—skiing was an upper-class holiday sport. Even today it is still very much a *sport.* It means dazzling dashes down the Swiss Alps. It has nothing to do with covering long distances fast over snow. The English reader will not make the connection between snow and skis (as a Norwegian would immediately) which would enable him to solve the crime.

Inevitably there are some few examples of miscalculation. The clue of the initial brooch seen in the mirror in *Dumb Witness* [U.S. *Poirot Loses a Client*] is one such: the reader certainly ought to see the significance of this—quite apart from the objection made (when the book was published) by the *Times,* arbiter in such matters, that ladies really do not go wandering around houses at night with brooches pinned to their dressing gowns. *Dumb Witness* [U.S. *Poirot Loses a Client*] is in fact the only classic Christie that ought to make the reader feel stupid if he fails to solve it. Elsewhere her touch with the deceptive potential of the objects and smells of everyday life is unerring: if Sherlock Holmes understands the significance of the dog *not* barking in the night, Agatha Christie understands the significance of a room *not* smelling of tobacco in the morning. One of her major strategies of deception springs from her ability to see and use the sinister possibilities behind things that the ordinary reader sees and handles every day of his life. That is part of the comfortable feeling he has when opening a Christie—that murder is being brought, deliciously, home to him.

VII

Three Prize Specimens

Hercule Poirot's Christmas
[U.S. *Murder for Christmas*]

The English house-party murder—the quintessentially English murder as far as many readers are concerned—is, as we have seen, not really Agatha Christie's cup of tea. On the other hand, there did come upon her periodically the urge to try her hand at an exercise in one of the classic modes or to exploit originally one of the classic situations of the detective story. *The Body in the Library* is the result of one such impulse. *Hercule Poirot's Christmas* is the result of another—a display piece on two traditional themes: the house-party murder and the locked-room murder. It is typical of Christie that this particular house party is not a smart-set affair: all the guests are "family," whether born on the right or the wrong side of the blanket. Except, of course, those who turn out to be impostors—another highly traditional ingredient in a tradition-bound recipe.

The Christmas of the title was no doubt a good selling point for the Collins list in 1938, but it is typical of Christie in her classic period that she exploits hardly at all the warm, cozy connotations of the season (just as it is typical of her later period that "The Adventure of the Christmas Pudding" becomes an exercise in nostalgia, with precious little hard detection in it at all). The bulk of the action takes place on Christmas Eve, Christmas Day and Boxing Day, yet we get practically no wistful mentions of turkey wasted, plum pudding untasted, or crackers unpulled, at least until near the end of the book—that is, when the serious business of clue-planting is over. There is hardly more than the most perfunctory remark about the inconvenience of a murder at Christmas, some nodding acknowledgment of its incongruity: everyone gets straight down to the job of interviewing the suspects and interpreting the clues. The puzzle is all.

And it is in the puzzle that *Hercule Poirot's Christmas*'s special distinction lies: in the planting of the clues, in the sleight of hand that conceals their true significance, in the double-edged remark that passes us by but registers with Poirot. The book is something of an exercise, and we should not look too closely at the mechanics of the murder, still less ask ourselves whether anyone in their senses would actually plan a murder as complicated and risky as this one. With this, more than with most Christies, one should throw realism out the window, accept the conventions of the genre, and sit back and enjoy it.

The characterization in this book is what one might call standard Christie: there are one or two stereotypes, several characters sketched in lightly but with no particular vividness, and one embryonic monster as victim—embryonic because (unlike, say, Mrs. Boynton in *Appointment with Death*) he is killed off before he can detract from the puzzle and overbalance the book by making too strong an impact on the reader's imagination. The stereotypes include a pompous, self-important and mean Conservative MP and his glamorous, vapid and greedy wife; a Spanish girl with all the traditional popular attributes—sultry, hot-blooded and vengeful; and Christie's usual stalwart colonial from (as usual) South Africa. He is (as everyone knows all colonials are) big, broad-shouldered, deeply suntanned, and with the inevitable determined jaw. But then jaws. . . .

Perhaps more characteristic of Christie's usual practice than these stereotypes are those characters where a gesture is made in the direction of a more complex style of characterization, though it is a gesture that is never carried very far. Here we have the devoted mother's boy who still resents her wrongs twenty years after her death and still nurses his boyhood resentment against his father. Then there are the ne'er-do-well and ne'er-do-ill sons, the one with a whole history of dubious transactions, the other a dogsbody who has always put his father's wishes and require-ments first, and perhaps has come to resent it. And so on, and so on. Someone whose literary allegiance is to the traditional novel, particularly in its great nineteenth-century manifestations, is likely to find these creations pallid and unstimulating. But, with-out wishing to anticipate the argument of my final chapter, it is possible to wonder how helpful expectations brought from this sort of reading are when brought to bear on the detective story. One might well argue that the strength of Christie's characteriza-tion lies in the fact that it is *enough*—not memorable, certainly, but just vivid enough for us to distinguish between the various sus-pects, maintain a mild interest in them as people, and above all *enough* to sustain the puzzle without distracting from it by turning our attention off on to something else—a study in morbid psy-chology, for example. For the Christie type of detective story the characterization has to be sufficiently convincing to arouse our interest in the puzzle, but it certainly must not be so detailed and particular that it distracts us from it. In her best books Christie manages to maintain this nice balance.

The basis of the deceptions practiced in *Hercule Poirot's Christmas* is the question of family resemblances and traits held in common by siblings. No less than two characters turn out to be illegitimate sons of the dead man, while another turns out to be not after all his grandchild as she has claimed. This last matter is elucidated by a simple dropping of the information that both her supposed parents were blue-eyed, while she is brown-eyed—a simple matter, but the placing of the relevant information is done with beautiful tact and skill. The matter of the illegitimate sons is put before us with an even greater cunning. The resemblances are drawn to our notice quite unemphatically, but they are mentioned over and over again: the arrogant jaw, the aquiline nose, and so on, together with a few characteristic gestures such as stroking the jaw with a forefinger. From early on the attentive reader is likely to notice that his attention is being directed to Stephen Farr and his physical presence—to the fact, for example, that the butler, opening the front door to him soon after doing the same for the ne'er-do-well son of the house, Harry, has a confusing sense of "I have been here before" (the Priestley play of that name is actually referred to obliquely). That same attentive reader may well from that moment start clocking up family resemblances between Stephen Farr and the sons of Simon Lee, and perhaps even congratulate himself on his sharpness—though in fact he is just responding to a detective-story cliché, the outsider who turns out to be quite other than what he claims to be. Agatha Christie often uses the presence of possible impostors as a way of sharing around the suspicion (e.g., in *Murder in Mesopotamia* or *Taken at the Flood* [U.S. *There Is a Tide*]) but it is usually marginal to the central problem, and one can be quite sure that if the solution to the murder *does* lie in an imposture (as in *Taken at the Flood*) that particular imposture will not be signaled so obviously or so early on in the detective process.

And while all this is going on, Christie is planting the *real* clues. It is a measure of her skill in doing double somersaults that these are mostly of precisely the same kind. We are told not once but four times of Superintendent Sugden drawing his finger along the line of his jaw—one of the family characteristics that Stephen Farr shares with half-brother Harry. It is just after Sugden has thrown back his head and laughed (another family characteristic much insisted upon) that Hercule Poirot feels he has seen a ghost. Above all Christie has arranged, again very unobtrusively, a series of confusions in her characters' minds between different characters which follow on from Tresillian the butler's initial bewilderment over the Harry/Stephen likeness, all done unemphatically as unimportant human errors:

"Mr. Harry was talking enough for twenty—no, not Mr Harry, the South African gentleman."

Or:

"Who's that out there in the garden? Superintendent Sugden, or Mr Farr?"

There are four or five such confusions, all of them merely conversational irrelevancies, it seems, and all in fact designed to establish that the dead man has *three* men in the house who resemble him and inherit his physical mannerisms: one acknowledged son, and two unacknowledged ones. Most cunning of all is the moment when Pilar Estravados shoves the resemblance under our noses yet we fail to pick up the by now all-pervasive scent. She says of the dead man:

"I liked him all the same. I think that when he was a young man, he must have been handsome—very handsome, like you," said Pilar to Superintendent Sugden. Her eyes dwelt with naive pleasure on his handsome face, which had turned brick-red at the compliment.

The reader inevitably falls into the trap of seeing this as the typical stolid Englishman's embarrassment at an overtly sexual compliment, and thus he fails to see that what is being offered is information, not a mildly comic point. The same technique is used in another much-quoted example of Christie's skill in clueing: Poirot asks Tresillian whether the wall calendar has been changed since the murder; Tresillian walks over and peers at it. The reader wonders over the significance of the date and whether it has been changed, whereas the real fact of significance is that Poirot hereby establishes the state of the butler's eyesight. As with the Farr–Harry–Sugden confusion, a card is forced on the reader while the author conceals the ace of trumps up her sleeve.

Of course, family resemblances do not make a court case, and Christie has to come up with something more concrete in the way of evidence, though it must be said that Christie's murderers, including this one, are in general much too apt to confess in the face of evidence that wouldn't convict a cat of stealing fish. Certainly one has doubts whether any British jury would convict a highly respected police superintendent on the basis of the peg-and-balloon clue in this story. Nevertheless its placing and use provide a typical example of Christie's cunning: we see Pilar Estravados pick it up, and register Superintendent Sugden's demanding it from her immediately after the discovery of the body; then we hear nothing about it until toward the end, when one of the characters slyly draws attention to it as a way of suggesting that Pilar Estravados was guilty of the murder; then Sugden produces it and confesses that he was totally baffled by it—"If you can make anything of it, I'll retire from the police force!" (as indeed, in a sense, he does). The reader's attention is drawn back to Pilar Estravados, and he ignores the truly startling fact that Sugden has been in possession of this baffling object from the beginning of the investigation without so much as mentioning it to his fellow investigators.

These are the main clues in the book; there are others equally well contrived. On two occasions Sugden suspiciously steers clear of subjects one would expect him to follow up: for example, when Alfred Lee repeats his father's reference to sons "born on the wrong side of the blanket," Sugden is "suddenly alert," and yet immediately asks a question on quite a different subject. There are some weaknesses too. The book has perhaps less sheer narrative drive than some other Christie books of the 'thirties. It gets a little bogged down in the central section by a series of Ngaio Marsh-y interviews on the subject of "Where exactly were you when the scream was heard?" Then again there is the problem of Christie's second murders, which will come up again in connection with *A Murder Is Announced.* Here it is only an attempted murder, but plot-wise it is an excrescence, and from a practical point of view totally ludicrous: you try murdering somebody by balancing a cannon ball on his door!

But all in all *Hercule Poirot's Christmas* is a highly superior example of Christie's habitual procedures in her classic phase: the plot is meticulously thought through, not a detail is misplaced or without significance in the total scheme, and above all the reader has that satisfying sense that the clues have all been fairly and squarely placed in front of him—even if he has somehow been induced to look out of the window at the crucial moment of placing.

Five Little Pigs
[U.S. *Murder in Retrospect*]

In 1942–43, sixteen years after the traumatic disappearance and divorce, Agatha Christie wrote *Five Little Pigs,* a book about a murder which had taken place sixteen years before, a murder springing from the classic triangular situation (wife, estranged husband, and the woman he is besotted with) which had precipitated that determining crisis in her own life.

No doubt it would be easy to make too much of this. No detailed scheme of resemblances would stand scrutiny: Archie Christie seems to have had little in common with the artist Amyas Crale except his initials and (conjecturally) his totally amoral devotion to himself and his pleasures of the moment; the young, pleasure-loving Agatha Christie seems to have had little in common with the neurotic Caroline Crale; and about the third component in the real-life triangle we know too little to form an opinion.

Yet there *are* enough parallels to make one feel that there is more than mere coincidence in that "sixteen years," whether or not Christie was herself conscious of them: in both cases a woman in her mid-thirties, with a decade or so of marriage behind her and a very young daughter, is told by her husband that he is leaving her for a younger woman. It is not surprising that in dealing with this (admittedly stereotyped) situation there emerges a degree of feeling and a psychological grasp unusual in Christie at any period in her career.

The starting point of the novel is this: Poirot is visited by a young woman, now known as Carla Lemarchant but in fact Caroline Crale the younger, who asks him to investigate the murder of her father, Amyas Crale the painter, sixteen years before, when she was a young child of five. Her mother, Caroline, had been convicted of the murder, but the death sentence was commuted, and she died some time afterward in prison.* The reason her daughter wants the case reopened has little to do with "heredity" or "bad blood"—always a danger point with Christie, and a subject on which she was inclined to talk (at least through her characters) a great deal of nonsense—but springs from a letter from her mother, given her on her twenty-first birthday, in which she assures her daughter of her innocence. There is also a feeling that doubt about this subject may poison the marriage on which she is about to embark. This is the point of departure for the first and best of a series of books in which Christie sets her sleuths to investigating a murder in the past.

The sense the reader has of unusual psychological depth to this novel springs partly from the unconventional shape of it: it is, in essence, a series of reports and memories of the long-ago murder

---

*In *Elephants Can Remember* she is said to have died before the execution could take place, which proves that elephants sometimes forget.

case by those involved either with the murder itself or with its investigation and prosecution. Thus we have (as in most of the best Wilkie Collins novels, but with the various reports much better motivated and explained) a multiple perspective on the events and the characters involved in them which gives an appearance of complexity even to characters which are basically drawn from Christie stock. And in the case of the central actors in the drama there is a degree of dramatic imagination and emotional sympathy at work which gives them a genuine (and unaccustomed in Christie) life and depth.

It is important to distinguish this investigation of a long-forgotten murder case from similar excursions late in Agatha Christie's writing life. There she uses the formula as an excuse to meander nostalgically among the objects and customs of the past; there the haziness of the characters' memories functions as a cover for her own slack grasp on the details of her plot. In other words, in those books the retrospective plot is both a self-indulgence and a cover. In *Five Little Pigs* she uses the time lag to make dramatic points about the consequences to the characters of their involvement in the case, and to create a genuine tension between "them-then" and "them-now." To take one example of this kind of tension: we hear about the actions of the young Elsa Greer from various points of view, both disapproving and admiring, but we can also bear in mind the bored society divorcée that we know she has become since the murder. This makes the final paragraph of the book, where she goes out to her chauffeur-driven car to live out the life of pampered emptiness she has made for herself, both impressive and, what is unusual in Christie, moving.

It is in fact in connection with Elsa Greer and the dead Caroline Crale that the multiple-perspective technique works most effectively. Right from the beginning, in the conversations with the policeman and the lawyers connected with the case, we are presented with a variety of interpretations of the triangular situation which is at the center of the case. On the one hand, Elsa is a ruthless sexual predator, taking what she wants without a moment's thought for the damage she is inflicting on others; on the other hand she is "young, ruthless, but horribly vulnerable," a girl whose life has been ruined by the death of her lover, Crale, and who has since been "only a somewhat mediocre young woman seeking for another life-sized hero to put on an empty pedestal." Throughout the book Christie maintains a tension between the cliché sentimentalizations of youth and the contrary view which sees it as crude, powerful and cruel, yet vulnerable from its lack of insight into emotional realities. The tension between the two sides of this double viewpoint is to be resolved effectively on the final page of the book.

It is through the multiple perspectives on the wife in the case, Caroline Crale, that Christie comes as close as she ever did to a rounded portrait. Contrasted with the vulnerable creature at the trial who could summon up no eloquence or self-defensive passion to plead her case, who seemed to want to be found guilty, is the "turbulent, unhappy creature" who in a fit of adolescent jealousy had permanently disfigured her baby sister.* This contrast too is to be effectively resolved by the solution of the mystery, and it is developed throughout the book by all the people who knew her. To Philip Blake, sexually attracted by her yet tormented by guilt feelings since she is the wife of his best friend, she appeared to use impulsiveness as a cloak for a calculating nature—she was a "cold egotistical devil." To his brother, Meredith, she is a put-upon saint. To the governess she is the victim of the eternal tyranny of man. Most effective of all is the analysis of her given us by her sister, the one whom she had injured and the one who understands best the emotional consequences to a passionate nature of committing such an act, which leaves behind an eternal witness to its bestiality. The fact that she had disfigured someone for life lies behind Caroline Crale's

---

*The dates and ages, always a weak point with Christie, especially later on, are not at all well worked out here. Caroline Crale could not be less than twenty when this happened.

every action, explains both the unnatural calm and repression of her habitual behavior and the only way open to her to let her passionate nature find some vent:

> She took her own ways of guarding against it [the impulse to violence]. One of these ways was a great extravagance of language. She felt . . . that if she were violent enough in speech she would have no temptation to violence in action.

All these sides to Caroline Crale are not only used to create a subtle and convincing character study: they are also to be used as contributory factors when the time comes to explain her actions and arrive at a solution to the mystery. In this book, to a much greater extent than is usual in Christie, character is solution.

Around these two characters cluster images from and references to hunting and blood sports. Partly these establish a frame of reference for the trial and conviction of Caroline Crale—establish the ambiguous nature of justice which Christie was willing to acknowledge at this stage in her career. "In the Central Criminal Court, as on the playing fields of Eton, and in the hunting country, the Englishman likes the victim to have a sporting chance," says the man who had been Counsel for the Prosecution at Caroline Crale's trial. Her passive, acquiescent demeanor in the face of the overwhelming evidence against her "appealed to chivalry—to that queer chivalry allied to blood sports which makes most foreigners think us such almighty humbugs." And he adds, apropos of Elsa Greer: "the judge didn't like her. Old Avis, it was. Been a bit of a rip himself when young—but he's very hot on morality when he's presiding in his robes." All the images, taken together, suggest very effectively, even scathingly, the moral duality of law and its enforcement, a duality which had been hinted at only a few years earlier in the conclusion to *Ten Little Niggers* [U.S. *And Then There Were None*]. In particular they establish a picture in our mind of Caroline Crale as the victim of a cruel sport who refuses to "play the game" by putting up a fight, leaving the spectator not exhilarated, as after an apparently equal fight, but nastily conscious of the eye-for-an-eye aspects—as well as the hypocrisy—of the judicial process.

One of the most striking of these blood-sports references is put into the mouth of Elsa Greer, and—though we don't know it at the time—it gains added significance from the fact that she says it as she watches her lover dying by her hand:

> "I think you're right about Spain. That's the first place we'll go to. And you must take me to see a bullfight. It must be wonderful. Only I'd like to see the bull kill the man—not the other way about. I understand how Roman women felt when they saw a man die. Men aren't much, but animals are splendid."

Meredith Blake adds: "I suppose she was rather like an animal herself—young and primitive and with nothing yet of man's sad experience and doubtful wisdom." The point is that we have been witnessing a bullfight, splendid and bloody, and Amyas Crale— the ruthless artist, and image of the showy matador—is being slain in the arena to which he descended of his own accord by the animal creature he has challenged.

There is another striking animal image for Elsa Greer when Crale, meeting her for the first time, tries to convey something of the effect she makes:

> "I've sometimes wanted to paint a flight of impossibly-coloured Australian macaws alighting on St. Paul's Cathedral. If I painted you against a nice traditional bit of outdoor landscape, I believe I'd get exactly the same result."

Elsa is a superb creature of nature, proud, flamboyant, instinctual —and the way is being prepared for the revelation of the instinctive animal revenge she takes when she finds that her desires have been thwarted.

This last quote from Amyas Crale suggests an aspect of the book that not even an admirer of Christie would expect. Crale is not perhaps a figure of any great depth—the amoral, wenching, life-loving artist who sacrifices anyone who stands in the way of his art. He is the conventional literary stereotype of a painter, and though undoubtedly effectively done within the stereotype, one must not expect a *Horse's Mouth* from Christie. On the other hand, he is given a degree of solidity and depth by Christie's success in describing his pictures: one is actually convinced of his extraordinary quality as an artist. And these pictures do more than establish the character of the man who painted them; they are also used to give depth to the characters of people who see them: for example two characters—Hale the policeman and Miss Williams the governess—are by implication diminished by their inability to appreciate the quality of Crale's vision.

There are several paintings mentioned, including one "amazing painful 'Nativity,'" but only two are actually described. One is a flowerpiece:

A vase of roses on a polished mahogany table. That hoary old set-piece. How then did Amyas Crale contrive to make his roses flame and burn with a riotous almost obscene life? The polished wood of the table trembled and took on sentient life. How explain the excitement the picture roused?

The second is the picture he is painting of Elsa Greer when he is killed, which he plans in his own mind thus:

"I'm itching and aching now to get at my brushes to see you sitting there on that hoary old chestnut of a battlement wall with the conventional blue sea and the decorous English trees —and you—you—sitting there like a discordant shriek of triumph."

That "riotous almost obscene life" of the roses, that "discordant shriek of triumph" which is Elsa, define very clearly the kind of animal vitality Amyas Crale feels akin to and can capture in paint, as well as telling us something about the woman who kills him. It is also writing of a vividness and style one might have thought quite out of Agatha Christie's range.

So far I have been talking as if this were a conventional novel about an artist and his women. In fact, it *is* the Christie detective story that most nearly approaches the novel proper, and it is probably the safest recommendation to anyone who doesn't like detective stories but would like to understand what people see in Agatha Christie. But *Five Little Pigs* is also a detective story, and a very good one, clearly in the classic line of her 'thirties and early 'forties successes. Fittingly, since this is a murder investigated in retrospect, we have few of the conventional types of clues here: all physical traces have long ago been destroyed, and for once Poirot's claim to be a detective who specializes in the psychological approach has some justification. What the reader has to attend to in particular in this book are the conversations, and he could well try reading them out aloud, for what he has to do is to capture tones of voice, register shades of meaning, allow for possible ambiguities. The solution depends on the way we interpret brief fragments of conversation or correspondence: "You and your women! I'd like to kill you"; "I'll see to her packing"; or "One has to pay one's debts." If one reads the various narratives sensitively, with the total situation and the emotional histories of the protagonists in mind, one has at least a chance of coming up with the solution.

In fact, rarely for Christie, the strength of the book is in the psychology and the clever use of perfectly natural conversation. The more concrete clues are less successful than usual: the jasmine clue is fair enough—the knowledge of when jasmine flowers is not too esoteric to rule it out of court—but it is far from vital to the solution. One other major clue rouses more doubts: the information, gleaned from the governess, that she *saw* Caroline Crale pressing her husband's hands on the beer bottle is dramatically effective: it is this that convinces Poirot that she could *not* have done the murder, since the poison was in the glass not the bottle, and she clearly did not realize this. However, at this point it is best to read on quickly and not think too hard, because it is difficult to believe that the police and defending counsel at the time would have failed to see the significance of this, or that—since Caroline Crale had believed her injured stepsister had tampered with the bottle, and was taking the rap for her—the accused herself would have failed to see the significance of the poison being in the glass rather than the bottle (she apparently died believing she had shielded her sister in an act of reparation for injuring her).

There are a few other weaknesses in the story: Meredith Blake's character never quite comes into focus, and the narration of a sexual episode between Philip Blake and Caroline Crale ("And then, with my arms round her, she told me quite coolly that it was no good") notably fails to convince; Christie wrote of her dislike of romance in detective stories, and would probably have put sex in the same category—as a distraction to be avoided wherever possible. The nursery-rhyme structure too is an excrescence on what is basically an exceptionally serious story.

Beyond that everything comes off: the minor characters—lawyers and policemen especially—are neatly and economically done; there is a feminist governess who is presented with a sympathy and good sense Christie does not always show when dealing with independently minded women (though she might have spared us the line "She was a great feminist and disliked men"); the writing is never less than competent and sometimes a good deal better than that. Compare the styles in which the various witnesses narrate their memories of the crucial days with the uniform and stilted prose in which most of the clients at Baker Street present their problems.

All in all, it is a beautifully tailored book, rich and satisfying. The present writer would be willing to chance his arm and say that this is the best Christie of all.

A Murder Is Announced

Agatha Christie was a writer with an enormous output—sometimes as many as three titles a year at her peak, and before she woke up to the fact that it didn't pay—and yet an astonishingly large number of her titles remain distinctly individualized in the average reader's memory. Often, as I have suggested, this memorableness is due to the staggering solution. Sometimes it is due to the setting, because though she is poor at individualizing places, and far from a mistress of atmosphere, nevertheless she did range more widely than her competitors and produce some splendidly original settings for mayhem—lots of trains, a plane, a riverboat, the South of France, Mesopotamia, Egypt ancient and modern. The only places one feels are oddly neglected are all parts of the British Isles outside London and the genteelly rural counties.

But as often as not the individualizing touch that makes her books stick in people's minds springs from her ability to conceive and work through "a good idea for a murder"—a circumstance which makes her crimes stand out from run-of-the-mill coshings and stabbings. Thus she has her nursery-rhyme murders, her ABC murders, her murders centered on games, and so on. These ideas, vivid though they are, usually remove her story even further than normally from any idea that they could be a realistic depiction of crime. She was an entertainer, seldom tried to be anything more, and she tried to center her entertainments on imaginative ideas that were nevertheless close to her readers' own everyday or, often, childhood experience.

These ideas certainly vary in quality. Where the nursery rhymes are apt, as in *Ten Little Niggers* [U.S. *And Then There Were None*] for example, they enhance the delight of the story. Where they are strained, or where the story is contrived to fit the details of the jingle—as in, say, *A Pocket Full of Rye* or *Hickory, Dickory Dock* [U.S. *Hickory, Dickory Death*]—they merely drag the novel down. Sometimes the idea is magnificent but the solution is a letdown—as with *The Clocks,* with its intriguing corpse surrounded by a multitude of clocks telling different times—an idea of which literally nothing is made in the conclusion of the story.

A Murder Is Announced is one of those Christies one remembers because she has taken something everybody is familiar with, an announcement of marriage, and used it creatively. "A marriage is announced" . . . "A murder is announced"—it is the sort of feeble wordplay one indulges in in idle moments of flicking through the duller parts of a newspaper, which may well be how it came to Christie's mind. She then, as usual in her best period, thinks the idea through magnificently: an announced murder—how would it be received? what would people do? and so on. And the "announced murder," when it duly takes place, is not only a memorable set-piece that gets the book moving at the double; it also provides the excuse for some gentle satire on smalltown inquisitiveness and sensation-seeking, some mildly sociological investigation of reading habits in small rural communities, and some good satire in the comedy-of-manners style as the middle ranks of Chipping Cleghorn assemble (with some nervousness and a great deal of embarrassment) in Miss Blacklock's drawing room at the appointed time, uncertain whether they are to expect murder in jest or murder in earnest.

One of the strengths of this book is the meticulous way Agatha Christie chronicles, and in particular the way she *uses,* the changing mores of her neck of the middle-class woods in the immediate postwar years. What we have here are not so much reduced gentlefolk—the sort of people whose plight she records with considerable understanding and devastating snobbery in "The Listerdale Mystery"—but gentlefolk faced with the aggressive threats to their position posed by an egalitarian age. There are many indications in this book that in 1950, in the age of Attlee, things are not what they used to be for the gentry and the near-gentry. Maids are a thing of the past, though the phenomenon of the daily who "does" for various households ensures an even speedier dissemination of village gossip. The old unity and cohesion of the middle class is breaking up: as Miss Marple comments, in the past the genteel inhabitants of the village would have been a stable group, and any newcomers would bear letters of introduction to one or other of the group, vouching for their gentility. The war has destroyed this cohesion, and now the village is populated by people who assert their middle-classness but who are not known to each other, or vouched for in any way. A feeling of class uncertainty is in the air.

On the other hand, there is a new sort of unity emerging, a unity born of adversity: as they fight, backs to the wall, against the prevailing egalitarianism, they certainly fight together. In an era of rationing and shortages, each middle-class family in Chipping Cleghorn has its own luxury-producing sideline—bees, chickens, fruit trees—and a lively barter system prevails among them. They form a sort of bourgeois collective, and because much of the bartering is of dubious legality they circumvent police snooping by having set hiding places for their produce and leaving houses always open to facilitate the exchange—one of the facts which Christie makes cunning use of.

This bartering is mostly a genial assertion of middle-class solidarity, but it can be abused by the grasping:

"That's not a fair exchange at all! Vegetable marrows are quite unsaleable at the moment—everybody has such a lot."
"Naturally. That's why Mrs Lucas rang up. Last time, if I remember rightly, the exchange suggested was some skim milk —*skim* milk, mark you—in exchange for some lettuces. It was then very early in the season for lettuces. They were about a shilling each."

The whole social panorama in *A Murder Is Announced* is done with a great deal of quiet assurance—and there is never much doubt in the reader's mind (or Christie's) that the hard-pressed middle class will consolidate their defenses and survive the austerities of Cripps and the aggressive forays of Bevan. A glorious restoration in the Tory 'fifties is just around the corner.

And if the novel capitalizes on the details of social intercourse in rural England in the postwar years, it makes equally good use of the domestic settings of her middle-class characters—in fact this is one of the best examples of Christie's ability to suggest menace and uncertainty under a cozy façade. The vital physical clues are all part of the everyday setup of bourgeois living: flowers that have died for lack of water, a burn on the table, table lamps that have been exchanged. The reader needs to pay attention to such details as why the central heating has been turned on, on the day of the first murder, yet coal fires are blazing when the time for the solution comes round. The eye for detail, and what can be made of it, is as sharp in Christie at this stage as it had ever been.*

And so is the ear. Like *Five Little Pigs,* [U.S. *Murder in Retrospect*] *A Murder Is Announced* gets some of its best effects from capitalizing on the shades of meaning that can be extracted from conversational banalities. It was not for nothing that Christie was very insistent that no interfering editor should render the speech of her characters more traditionally grammatical than it was when it left her hand.** A great deal depends on the naturalness and flow of the dialogue—for in the ease of reading lies the best hope of concealing the vital clues. This is particularly evident in the speech of the companion, Dora Bunner.

This is a sketch on which Christie lavished a great deal of care —understandably, since she is central to the elucidation of the problem. In the skill with which suspicion is on occasion directed at her through her love of "nice things" we probably see the germ

---

*One slight doubt, though: are violets likely to be picked in the average garden at the end of October?

**But was it a pedantic gremlin in Collins that put into the mouth of a policeman the question: "Are these they?"

of the idea which became *After the Funeral.* [U.S. *Funerals Are Fatal*]
But the major triumph is the way Christie conveys an appearance
of skattiness while at the same time slipping all the vital information into her dialogue: it is *because* she is skatty that she cannot
conceal the truth—and it is *because* she loves "nice things" that her
observation of the all-important domestic details is to be relied
upon. Most skillful of all is her long, rambling conversation with
Miss Marple in the local teashop: here Christie creates intention-
ally a bewilderment in the reader which he tends to shrug off as
the result of Miss Bunner's woolly-mindedness, but which in fact
is the result of her simultaneously talking about two different
people without being able to reveal that this is what she is doing.

Which leads us to the best clues of all, which really are typo-
graphical—Christie relying on our reactions to the printed word as
an instrument of deception. Having by now triumphantly clocked
up fifty titles there was nothing Christie did not know about the
way people read popular literature. She knew that if Dora Bunner's affectionate diminutive for Letitia Blacklock—"Letty"—now
and again changed to "Lotty," eighty percent of her readers simply
would not notice. And nineteen of the remaining twenty would
assume it was a misprint, even if it occurred several times to
establish the fairness of the clue. (It should be said that misprints
are so frequent in some of the recent paperback reprints of Christie
books that the modern reader stands at a particular disadvantage
in relation to this clue.) Similarly with another clue: not one reader
in a thousand will notice whether a word is spelled *enquiries* or
inquiries, though Christie is quite justified in saying that this is a
matter in which a mature person's usage is likely to remain constant. For the rest, the reader must be as attentive as he knows how
for conversational nuances, particularly in the dialogues of Miss
Blacklock and Dora Bunner, and must meditate on the possible
inflections of such perfectly ordinary lines as "She wasn't there."

The success of the Dora Bunner part in this book does not stand
alone: Letty Blacklock is splendidly realized, an impressive pres-

ence with depths one senses but cannot analyze. And if many of the rest are drawn from the Christie repertory, it is worth noting what splendid potential there is there, waiting for the right actor, or more often actress, to take over the part in an adaptation and pump it full of vigorous caricature life. This happened in one case in the recent film of *Murder on the Orient Express* (Ingrid Bergman doing glorious things with the Swedish missionary lady, surrounded by a host of rather blank star appearances), and in several performances in *Death on the Nile,* where the producer had signed up a whole host of experienced cameo players. In *A Murder Is Announced* there is a wonderful little sketch, quite gratuitous, of Phillipa Haymes's employer, a woman with all the congenital acquisitiveness and bossiness of her class without the attendant acceptance of responsibilities or any feeling of solidarity with her own kind. There is also a lot of good dialogue lavished on, for example, the bored, glamorous young Julia, the public-school leftie Edmund Sweetenham, the elderly lesbian couple* and so on. Christie's dialogue is often more lively and effectively dramatic in the novels than in the stage plays. There is, however, one spectacular exception to this in Mitzi, the home help from Central Europe —a refugee who is treated with a typically Christiean lack of compassion ("It's been my experience in dealing with aliens that lying comes more easy than truth telling," says one of the policemen), and who is given dialogue that veers wildly from "stage-foreign" to totally idiomatic English. As far as foreigners were concerned, Christie was only really at home with French speakers.

For two-thirds of its length *A Murder Is Announced* is as good as Agatha Christie ever wrote. In the last fifty pages it suffers a damaging collapse into something approaching absurdity. For me

---

*Done sympathetically, but one of very few examples of sexual aberration in Christie. A fairly obvious homosexual in "Three Blind Mice" is the only other example that springs to mind. Men described as "effeminate" are usually only too interested in girls—in a nastily un-English way.

the collapse is symbolic, because the book seems to mark the end of Christie's classic period, those years when one could expect something satisfying, puzzling and entertaining from her. After 1950 one could only *hope:* there were some splendid successes, but they were interspersed with performances of embarrassing feebleness. She could still write something as good as *Mrs. McGinty's Dead,* but she could also put her name to the dreadful *Hickory, Dickory Dock,* with its preposterous plot and its shame-making caricatures of overseas students.

But this, of course, is to give undue symbolic weight to the (comparative) falling apart of *A Murder Is Announced.* What happens here is by no means unknown even in the classic period: she abuses the "impostor" ploy she has used over and over again, and she abuses the "second murder" ploy. It is all very well to bring in the red herring of the twins Pip and Emma as a means of diverting attention from the really important imposture, but by the end the search for possible pretenders resembles the aftermath of the slaughter at Ekaterinburg: practically the whole of Letitia Blacklock's household is found to be other than what it has claimed to be.

The second murder was a recurrent hazard with Christie, as we have seen in connection with *Hercule Poirot's Christmas* [U.S. *Murder for Christmas*]. Basically it springs from her uneasiness with the length expected of a detective story by publishers and public in her time. We learn from *An Autobiography* that she herself preferred around fifty thousand words, while her publishers expected ten or twenty thousand more—hence the second murders, which both pumped a bit of extra excitement into the business of detection, as well as prolonging the story. As Mrs. Oliver says in *Cards on the Table:* "when I count up I find I've only written thirty thousand words instead of sixty thousand, and so then I have to throw in another murder and get the heroine kidnapped again. It's all very boring" [chapter 17]. But here the matter gets quite out of hand, with two additional murders and one murder attempt (by a mur-

derer who is subsequently described as "kind"). This last is under-
taken in the kitchen while the police are in the drawing room, and
it is foiled by Miss Marple imitating the voice of the dead Dora
Bunner—a ploy as embarrassing as watching John Gielgud appear
in variety. For if Agatha Christie's Miss Marple is not quite a lady,
she is never less than ladylike.

VIII

A Note about Detectives

Mr. Satterthwaite, the human aide first to the semisupernatural Mr. Harley Quin and later to Hercule Poirot, is described as one whose "role had always been that of the onlooker." It is a phrase that might well be applied to all Agatha Christie's detectives: to Mr. Parker Pyne and Harley Quin, in the short story collections that bear their name, and above all of course to Hercule Poirot and Miss Marple. They are all solitaries: they watch other people, always benevolently, but always detached; they generalize about life, but they do not experience it directly; they have no loves or hates, nor ever have had; people confide their affairs to them, but they do not involve them emotionally; they watch life through windows, often through binoculars.

The exceptions, of course, are Tommy and Tuppence, but they are jolly adventurers rather than detectives.

In this detachment the typical Christie detective allies himself with Sherlock Holmes and, say, the Old Man in the Corner, rather than with the detective creations of any of Christie's British contemporaries. Lord Peter, Roderick Alleyn, Albert Campion all love, court and marry, usually over several books, and always women they have met in the course of investigating a crime. That fact alone proves the possibility of their being involved emotionally in a case—that it is not (as Christie preferred it to be in her books) purely a test of reason. In addition, they are all felt to be part of an ongoing life: they all have mothers, brothers and sisters, and a recognizable (and high) place in the social hierarchy—at least if they choose to assert it. This is not true of Christie's sleuths (or, interestingly, of the Chandler/Ross Macdonald type of detective). In spite of Poirot's long service with the Belgian police force one never gets a sense of him as a man with a past, still less as a man with a vital personal life in the past. He exists only in the present, he has function rather than character. Both he and Miss Marple are essentially middle-class figures, but, being single and childless, they do not have the same stake in the social system (the *existing* social system) as Lord Peter and the rest, who all have children— notably, who all have *sons,* heirs.

Of course, they do have relationships of a sort. In particular, Poirot in the early years has Hastings, as Holmes had Watson; but in neither case does any real warmth of friendship or feeling of identity of interests establish itself. The suggestion (made jocularly, one hopes) that the friendship of Poirot and Hastings is a very *special* sort of friendship rings even less true than similar innuendoes about the Holmes–Watson relationship. At least Holmes is very much a figure of the 'nineties, and the suggestion gains a certain plausibility from the historical context (however impossible to justify from the text). Poirot has no such context, nor can one begin to think in terms of a sexual life for him and Hastings. In fact, one cannot imagine Poirot getting Hastings to understand what homosexuality was.*

*Lew Archer's sexual inclinations, on the other hand, are surely due for investigation.

The rejection of Hastings from the Poirot saga in the 1930s is an interesting proof of how well Christie understood the demands of her story-telling craft. The drawbacks to the Poirot–Hastings partnership have in part already been hinted at. There was in this relationship no capacity for growth. Christie could only repeat—repeat Hastings's obtuseness and asininity, his superficial judgment of people and his partiality to women with auburn hair, his inevitable wrongness (which in itself tended to limit the openness of the cases he was involved with). And repeat on the other side Poirot's amused condescension, his kindergarten treatment of his friend and partner, which could so easily become not just monotonous, but also unpleasing.

Nor did Hastings function particularly well as storyteller, as the public chronicler of Poirot's famous victories. There is something slightly wooden about Conan Doyle's narrative style that consorts well with Watson's character—just as Doyle's own public persona was eminently Watsonian. There was no such identity possible between Agatha Christie and Captain Hastings. And the Watson-figure as narrator had a real disadvantage that may have been a factor in Conan Doyle's variable success with the longer form: he can only narrate a case naturally from the moment it becomes a case—that is, from the time it is brought to the Great Detective's notice. Now, the typical form of a Christie novel is to have a considerable lead-up to the murder, and this form corresponds well to the average reader's demands of a detective story: he wants to take in the setting, the surrounding circumstances, the characters who will be suspects; he wants, above all, to become interested in the corpse before it becomes a corpse. With a Watson-narrator this can only be done by resorting to one or other of various narrative expedients which can destroy the flow and unity of the story.

And the other reason why Hastings had to go is surely that he had no function in the main business of a detective story, that is, in the process of investigation. Watson is around for the strong-arm stuff—which Conan Doyle enjoyed but Christie had no use for; Magersfontein Lugg provides the underworld contacts whenever Campion needs to swerve beyond the boundaries of the law; Bunter and Foxkin chat up the ladies below stairs; Sergeant MacGregor does all the work Inspector Dover is too lazy to do himself. But Hastings has no such well-defined role to play. Hastings just trails along.

So Hastings had to go. In his place, as the occasion demanded, Christie used Poirot's valet, George, or his secretary, Miss Lemon, to represent unintelligent common sense, Mr. Satterthwaite to provide the social gossip, or Ariadne Oliver for comic relief. But after 1937 (with the exception of *Curtain,* intended as a requiem performance) Poirot is allowed to be what in essence he always has been: a solitary.

With Miss Marple, Agatha Christie did not make the same mistake: she has no friend, only a sort of entourage. Of these the most frequently mentioned is her nephew Raymond—a sort of Hugh Walpole figure who begins by being the darling of the avant-garde and ends up as a popular best-selling novelist. He seems to be quite obsessively fond of his aunt. Apart from him the entourage consists mainly of policemen and chief constables—professionals whom Miss Marple has acquired over the years, mere names whose function in the story is to express admiration and affection, nothing more.

Admiration in the early years, affection later on. Because over the years Miss Marple changes radically. Her publishers, in one of their blurbs, describe her as "fluffy," and her development is essentially a process of fluffification. She springs (as Christie herself acknowledged) from Caroline Shepherd, the sister of Dr. Shepherd in *The Murder of Roger Ackroyd,* one of her best-realized minor characters, and one of her own favorites. She is sharp-eyed, sharptongued, a vicious gossip with an incomparable information service and a desire to believe the worst. Miss Shepherd, however, was hardly smart at spotting murderers, even when they were on her own doorstep, or closer. In *The Murder at the Vicarage* she is recreated as Miss Marple, with that one talent added. Miss Marple's gardening is a smokescreen for her insatiable curiosity about the goings-on in her neighbourhood, her bird-watching is the ultimate length that curiosity can carry her to, and though she is admittedly described as having "a gentle, appealing manner," she is also called by one of the characters "a nasty old cat," which her general conduct and opinions throughout the book seem amply to justify.

But over the years the binoculars are put away, the gardening becomes a genuine rather than just a convenient passion, the gentle, appealing manner becomes a real guide to her human qualities rather than a smokescreen. She becomes a wise and charming old lady with no more than a mildly caustic view of human nature, whose detective ability springs less from her insatiable snoopiness than from her lengthy experience of the petty crimes and mysteries of village life. She becomes sweet.

It is worth noting that all Christie's major sleuths are unofficial ones—Miss Marple more so than Poirot, obviously, but though he can work with the police, be called in by them on occasion, nevertheless he is not of them. This means that Christie can take advantage of the private investigator's independence, which places him on the side of the law, but not part of it: thus, at the conclusion of the story, he can do things that a policeman could not do—wink at the culprit's suicide, decide he has suffered enough, even act as God and decide his crime was justified and craves no penalty.

There is no doubt that most Christie addicts prefer Miss Marple as a detective to Hercule Poirot, but in fact she was a much less useful figure. Being an amateur, she had to encounter murder: it could seldom be brought to her, nor she summoned to solve it. This meant that most of her murders had to be Mayhem Parva murders, at least until the final phase, when she was whisked around the world in a distinctly surprising manner. Nor is she in any rigorous sense a detective at all. Her cases are much more loosely organized affairs than Poirot's: they are solved less by clues and scrupulous reasoning from them than by intuition and village parallels. At the end of a Miss Marple book the villain tends to be brought to confess by a trick, or he commits suicide, or he is killed by another character. It is rare for Miss Marple actually to have anything that could be described as proof of anyone's guilt—something that could be produced in court in order to make a case. It is all, compared to Poirot at his best, terribly homely and easygoing. That is probably why Miss Marple is used sparingly in the classic phase, much more frequently in the later phases, when the rigorous thinking-through increasingly goes by the board.

Poirot, on the other hand, though undoubtedly irritating at times, and more a confection of quirks, whims and speech-oddities than a recognizable character, has justly earned his place as the best-known detective in twentieth-century crime fiction. Though he frequently claims to despise footprints, magnifying glasses and the whole business of detective fieldwork, and boasts of being able to solve crimes by sitting back and thinking, he is in fact completely versatile, and can frequently be found engaged in activities of a Holmesian kind—examining the grease spot on the carpet, remarking on the disarrangement of ornaments on the mantelpiece. On the other hand, though, some of his best cases are indeed superb examples of "thinking through"—notably *Cards on the Table* and *Death on the Nile*—and his orderly habits of thought and his passion for order around him seem to have stimulated Christie to turn in meticulously planned performances. He fails when he is involved with farragoes about master criminals (for example, Christie badly compromised his dignity by putting him into the dreadful *Big Four*), and is at his best when his cases bear "some relation to things as they happen" (*Peril at End House*, chapter 9). He himself mocks the *Moonstone* type of plot, with its "revengeful priests," and complains that the Sherlock Holmes stories are "in reality far-fetched, full of fallacies and most artificially contrived." It is certainly true that all those epithets could be applied to some of Poirot's own cases, but the very best ones are those like *Five Little*

Pigs [U.S. *Murder in Retrospect*], where there are no absurdities like guns hidden in hedges so as to go off when the gardener clips there.

That complaint just quoted about Sherlock Holmes is presumably an echo of the author's own opinion, since it repeats something said many years earlier by one of her alter egos, the comic figure of Mr. Clancy, the detective-story writer in *Death in the Clouds* [U.S. *Death in the Air*], who fulminates against "the fallacies—the really amazing fallacies there are in those stories." He also comments in a superior fashion: "Interesting, by the way, how the technique of the idiot friend has hung on," which is rich, coming from the creator of Hastings.

The crime writers in Christie are a rather interesting topic. For the most part they are alter egos used by Christie to reflect unseriously on the business of crime writing or on the merits or otherwise of the classic crime writers. There is Mr. Eastwood in "Mr Eastwood's Adventure" (*The Listerdale Mystery* [U.S. *Mystery of the Spanish Shawl*]) who thinks up fascinating titles and then invents stories to fit them, "though ten to one," he reflects, "[the editor] will alter the title and call it something rotten like 'Murder Most Foul' without so much as asking me!" (This reflection was perhaps prompted by the fact that her American publisher had recently started giving her books new titles. Ironically, many years later one of the Margaret Rutherford travesties of Miss Marple was given exactly that "rotten" title.)

Then there is the zany, manic figure of Mr. Clancy, by far the most entertaining of these figures to my mind, and with obvious resemblances to the alter ego Christie was most fond of and who most resembled herself, Mrs. Oliver. (Mr. Clancy eats bananas where Mrs. Oliver eats apples.) Ariadne Oliver reflects not only Agatha Christie's personal habits, even becoming teetotal over the years, but she also shares her fear of her public, her distrust of the whole public-relations machine and her lack of impressment with her own writings and the fame they have brought her. And of course there is also the fact that she is burdened with her dreadful Finn as her detective, though according to Poirot (in *The Clocks*, chapter 14) "it is clear she knows nothing about Finns or Finland except possibly the works of Sibelius," which must surely reflect Mrs. Oliver's creator's growing boredom with that odd product of the influx of Belgian refugees in the 1914–18 period.

Mrs. Oliver was useful, particularly in the later period, as a means of counteracting the cold rationality of Poirot, and the heartless regularity of his world and his approach to life. It is possible that, since she was—the skatty feminism apart—so easily recognizable as a comic version of the author herself, she was a means of softening the hard, cold persona which was all Christie could offer as a public image. Poirot represented that side of her nature—the cold, withdrawing side—and he flourished during that period when that side was uppermost, in particular during the two decades following the disappearance. In later years Mrs. Oliver could dilute his rationality with a warmer, more cheerfully disorganized kind of humanity. Miss Marple was always a rather more human character than Poirot: if she was, like Poirot, basically an observer of life, she still allowed herself, in later manifestations, much more warmth and feeling in the way she regarded the frailty and failings of others, and so came to embody the impulsive and generous sides of her author's nature.

But it is the cold, rational side that writes the best detective stories.

IX

Counsel for the Defense

Everyone who reads the traditional type of detective story, whether casually or addictively, will be familiar with the sort of objection to Agatha Christie and her kind voiced by Edmund Wilson, Bernard Levin and others, for they are only rehearsing the kind of argument heard over and over from people who do not respond to the appeal of the mystery story and are bewildered or irritated by their immunity. Most enthusiasts are somewhat at a loss as to how to counter such arguments: on the one hand, they sense how difficult it is to defend Christie and her contemporaries on their accusers' chosen grounds; on the other, they have a vague sense that, however reasonable the grounds may sound, these accusers are somehow missing the point, and that the sort of appeal these writers have for an enormous and devoted public rests on quite different foundations.

This latter feeling is, it seems to me, healthy and right. The attacks do miss the point, and they miss it very often because they bring to Christie all the preconceptions about what a novel should be which accumulate in the minds of those whose reading is mainly in the great eighteenth- and nineteenth-century classics of fiction. What they are saying is that *as novels* these works are beneath contempt: they look for solidly realized character drawing, for psychological depth, for evocative descriptions of settings; they look, even, for some "criticism of life," some statement about the human condition. And when inevitably they come back empty-handed from their search they come to the conclusion that life is too short to fritter away their time on such a trivial, feebleminded means of wasting time.

But in fact they are like a man who prospects for gold in a coal field. The first thing to get clear, in approaching Agatha Christie and her fellows, is that, by approaching them as novelists and by looking for the same sort of qualities one may hope to find in novels, these critics are making a mistake which prejudices the issue right from the start. Crime writers are not trying to write *Crime and Punishment.* Agatha Christie is a teller of popular tales, and should be judged by criteria appropriate to such a genre.

It is never very sensible to act as an evangelist for the detective story: if someone says, "I've never been able to acquire a taste for crime fiction—who do you recommend I try?" the sensible answer probably is, "Don't bother. If you have tried and you haven't responded, then probably the response isn't in you." The problem, for such readers, is usually that they "can never lose the taste of the construction," as Trollope said of some early examples of the form. And the problem is never likely to be resolved. On the other hand, it is reasonable, I think, to go on to suggest that he ought to try thrillers, or science fiction, or historical romances, or love stories—one or other of the branches of popular fiction. Because it *is* a pity to have become so sophisticated in one's reading that one can no longer thrill to a line like "Mr Holmes, it was the footprint of a gigantic hound!" or even "With a happy sigh she melted into his arms." Because to have lost the power to make these basic responses is to have lost the elementary response to fiction as *story.*

It is relevant here to look at the approach to the detective story of the French-American critic Jacques Barzun, one of the most voluminous and stimulating writers on the genre. One would like to be able to say one of the most influential as well, but in fact his writings have constituted an example of that most lonely and heroic of struggles—a battle against the fashionable tide. In article after article, and in his extraordinary *Catalogue of Crime,* he has elevated the authors of the classical whodunnit and deplored the shift in critical interest toward the realistic novel of crime—in particular the tough thriller-detective school of Hammett, Chandler and their pale equivalents in Great Britain. Where the critical orthodoxy today is to elevate this group to a lonely eminence, to see in Hammett and Chandler convincing diagnoses of the deep social malaises inherent in American capitalism, to praise the psychological insights of a Highsmith or a Symons, Barzun, in a series of splendid and idiosyncratic tirades, dissents: "the genre has not grown up, has not 'become literature': it has lost its aim and possibly its place in literature. It has ceased to give entertainment and has proffered nothing in exchange."

Strong stuff. And in the most thoroughgoing of his investigations into the appeal and the place of the detective story—an article called "The Novel Turns Tale"—Barzun has related his lifelong devotion to the genre to another preoccupation, what he sees as the exhaustion of the nineteenth-century concept of the novel. The bourgeois novel of character, of the Protestant conscience facing up to moral decisions in a massively detailed social context, of analytical studies of individuals and their dilemmas—this tradition had done all it could usefully do by the early twentieth century. It was played out, and if it did not die it could only repeat itself without the old exuberance or conviction. The only way the art of fiction could renew itself was by going back to older models, by seeking its inspiration, in fact, in the *tale* as opposed to the novel.

In the tale, closely allied to legend, fairy story, folk narratives and such like, the emphasis was fair and square on the storytelling elements, on seizing the reader's interest by incidents that might be thrilling, romantic, supernatural, totally fabulous. And this emphasis marks it off most definitely from the old realistic tradition of the novel, weighed down with character analyses and elaborate "atmosphere," in which the story often becomes no more than a regrettable necessity: "Oh dear yes," as Forster sighed, "the novel tells a story."

Thus Barzun stands out against the whole trend of recent writing on crime fiction which takes as its starting point the opening of Chandler's essay "The Simple Art of Murder," the patently untrue statement that "Fiction in any form has always intended to be realistic," and has thus viewed the crime story as limping fifty years late along the highway of realism, making its judgments and its critical distinctions on the basis of this shaky proposition.

One doesn't have to agree with all Barzun's contentions—with such a glorious tilter at windmills it would be patently impossible —to find this the most stimulating answer yet given to the problems presented by the detective story. I myself cannot see it as the reinvigorator of fiction, the successor to the novel proper: in fact the 'sixties and 'seventies seem to me to have been pretty good decades for the dear old bourgeois novel of the individual conscience, and there is something absurd about seeing a Dick Francis or an Alistair Maclean riding to the rescue of a tradition enfeebled to the point of a Drabble or a Lessing. Nor would I go along with another of Barzun's strong prejudices, his insistence on *detection* as the be-all and end-all of the detective story. This insistence is very strong in his *Catalogue of Crime,* and leads to some very odd judgments: how can one warm to a writer who despises Margery Allingham's Lugg, for example? In fact the detective formula has shown that it can embrace—in fact always has embraced—a lot more styles and approaches than Barzun would give it credit for, including the approach of the "hard-boiled" school.

But where I am sure he is right is in his insistence that we must cut off the modern detective story from the novel proper, put it in quite another category, one with its own traditions, conventions and demands, and thus develop a completely independent critical approach to it. I feel, in fact, that however we react to the novels of the American hard-boiled school, nothing but harm can be done by an attempt to see them as "realistic," or closer to the novel proper than other varieties of crime fiction. One hears so often these days the pronouncement that of course *detective* stories are trivial, escapist, utterly played out as a tradition, but that Chandler (or, more recently and incomprehensibly, Hammett) is another thing entirely. And the unwary general reader who acts on this cliché judgment and goes to Chandler or Hammett for the first time tends to come back with a puzzled frown on his face and an incipient shrug in his shoulder: what was all the fuss about? The same sort of misguided intellectual snobbery, seeking to make crime fiction respectable by making it what it is not, lies behind the judgment on Ross Macdonald, made by William Goldman in the *New York Times Book Review,* and which his English publishers use on the cover of paperback reprints: "One of the best American novelists now operating." The absurdity of such a pronouncement surely does not need underlining, and it nicely illustrates the harm we do to crime writers by using the novel proper as a way of placing them critically. If we insist that Chandler is a novelist, to be judged by putting him side by side with, say, Hemingway, Scott Fitzgerald or Sinclair Lewis, then one is forced to conclude that, however beautifully he may write, his plots are repetitive and intolerably clumsy, his characterization is superficial, his settings are monotonously sleazy and his "world view" a series of childish oversimplifications.

Nor will the much-touted "realism" of the hard-boiled school stand up to any very stringent examination. Books that concentrate their attention exclusively on gangsters, whores, and the corrupt superrich are every bit as partial in their scope and remote from the average reader's experience as books that concentrate on the genteel middle classes in the rural parts of Great Britain. If Christie has her stereotyped Anglo-Indian colonels and acidulated spinsters, how often do we meet in works of the California school the sexy middle-aged blonde with lust in her eyes and Martini on her breath? And if the average British policeman may blink at the goings-on of the investigators and the specimens of "detection" offered in the average Christie story, one wonders whether a real-life private eye in the Los Angeles or San Francisco area will really feel a shock of recognition when he reads of the doings of a Philip Marlow or a Lew Archer.

No one would deny that the best of the hard-boiled school put up a better *appearance* of realism than a Christie or a Marsh, and hide more skillfully their reliance on popular fiction clichés. But it is only a skin-deep realism, as any comparison with a genuinely realistic novelist like Dreiser or Sinclair Lewis must show. Ross Macdonald's stories are plotted in a tight-knit, convoluted way, so that every incident and every person, however casually, met on Lew Archer's despondent quest through the Golden State turns out to be integral to the solution of the problem he is engaged on at the moment. He cannot pick up a hitchhiker or turn off into a motel without thereby acquiring a vital piece in the whole elaborate, linked-up puzzle which is a Macdonald plot. This is not a criticism—quite the reverse. Macdonald's plots are magnificently conceived, satisfyingly shaped, and splendidly entertaining. But they haven't got much to do with realism. And is California really so jampacked with adolescents who have witnessed a murder in their infancy?

If we stop trying to force Chandler, Macdonald and the rest (admittedly on their own insistence) into a mode that is totally uncongenial, that of the realistic novel, and try to see them as, like Christie, tellers of tales, then their quality becomes much more apparent: both embody personal myths about the destruction of innocence and the corrupting effects of great wealth and power* in a series of highly wrought but exciting tales. They convey their vision by stereotyped characters and repetitive settings, which are given force by the obsessiveness of their private myth. What we read has only a marginal relation to the real world: it convinces us because it is a finely imagined fictional world, entire in itself, like the worlds of Tolkien or Peake, like the London of Dickens or the gloomy, hostile settings of the Gothic novelists. Or, of course, like the worlds of the English detective-story writers of the Golden Age. *The Big Sleep* looks much better in relation to *Clouds of Witness* or *The ABC Murders* than it does in relation to *The Great Gatsby.*

Because, in spite of differences of approach and ideology, the American and English crime writers are all writing thrillers,** and all writing in the tradition of the *tale* rather than the novel. *Roger Ackroyd* is not a failed *Middlemarch,* and nothing but confusion results from trying to judge it by the same criteria. It is a work in a tradition which includes the Gothic novel, Elizabethan prose fiction, *Robinson Crusoe,* the tales of Boccaccio, *Dr. Jekyll and Mr. Hyde, The Picture of Dorian Gray* and a whole host of works which writers on "the novel" feel uneasy about, can't decide whether or not to include in their surveys, can't find categories within which to subsume them. Anyone who comes back to the Sherlock Holmes

---

*The infrequency with which the private eye in American crime fiction gets paid, alluded to earlier, highlights an inherent contradiction in the genre: the society in which these softshoes move is capitalistic, vulgar and corrupt; yet it is the successful floaters on this scum who can afford to hire the private eye. The authors attempt a phony resolution of this contradiction (and incidentally endow the private eye with additional elements of the disinterested knight errant) by never letting him receive more than a basic fifty dollars a day, if that. Poirot, we imagine, on the other hand, sends in a meticulously detailed and exorbitantly high bill to his clients. They are well heeled but far from corrupt, and he has done them a service. No contradiction exists.

**The *alikeness* of all these forms of thriller is insisted upon and finely analyzed by Jerry Palmer in *Thrillers* (1978).

stories long after their childhood reading of them must surely get the vividest sense of their distinction—combined with an uneasy feeling that his habitual novel-reading has not given him the tools with which to analyze that distinction. The usual ones won't do: one can't deny the flatness of much of the writing, the four-squareness of the characterization, the conventionality of the moral code. And yet. . . .

It should surprise no one that the detective story should be so like the novel and yet should have its own rules and demands, which make a quite different yardstick necessary in judging it. One might cite an analagous case from another art. The opera singer who is hailed as a "great actress" would probably be tittered off stage if she took to acting with a provincial rep. Callas's way was that of a *singing-actress,* and her Violetta in *Traviata* would be totally unacceptable if it were transplanted into *La Dame aux Camellias.* Christie's procedures in *Roger Ackroyd* may look threadbare if we try to think of it as a novel, but they were right for a detective story.

The reasons why a Christie novel is so absorbing to so many hinge on her abilities as a storyteller and on the skill with which she mingles all or most of the ingredients of the main popular literary forms. Romantic interest, as we have seen, is no more than an incidental part of her books,* and is treated very coolly: the reader is *not* encouraged to commit himself totally to the romantic experience offered. Excitement occupies a rather larger share of the interest, though her books can only nominally be included under the umbrella title "thrillers": in general they do not thrill. But she does manage the "big scene" in a way to involve or excite the reader, and she dots her books with stupendous revelations or

---

*The thriller formula can accommodate sex more easily than the whodunnit, but even there it tends to be either mechanized, "status-seeking" copulation, or a variety of the "good-chums" relationship (as strong today in a writer like Desmond Bagley as in the days of John Buchan).

bursts of action which keep the reader in a state of compulsive attention.

But the basis of Christie's success as a popular writer is the way she structures her books on a pattern of progressive mystification and progressive enlightenment. In the sections leading up to the murder the reader's interest is held by the gradual revelation of vital elements in the murder situation—though the revelation is frequently misleading, as we have seen, and thus mystification and enlightenment go hand in hand. They do too in the succeeding sections, in that she reveals information that has the effect of still further complicating the initial problem. But all these apparent complications are to be used in the final section when they fall together to form a total elucidation of everything that has hitherto baffled us. This structure of mystification and enlightenment is the basis of the excitement and the readability of a Christie story: not (as in a real thriller) a succession of incidents leading to a climax, but a progressive giving of information which eventually is to fall in place to form a total picture which illumines both the initial murder situation and the incidental mystifications of the actual killing. This total picture may have been there from the beginning, but obscured from the reader because the necessary information was fragmented or misplaced. The excitement of the book (and in this a Christie plot is little different from, say, a Ross Macdonald plot) lies in the ordering of this fragmentary information to form a recognizable and convincing whole.

Thus, she is not writing the sort of story which is character in action—where what happens must seem to spring inevitably from what the characters are, as in *Middlemarch* or *Portrait of a Lady*. She is writing a story where facts and incidents are of prime importance, and where characters must be tailored to suit them. She understood instinctively that the character interest of her stories had to be subordinate to her puzzles, must never be allowed to get out of hand. In this, as in so much else, she learned from Conan Doyle, whose characters flicker in brief, sufficient life on the printed page and then are forgotten. There is a fine character study inherent in what we are told about Professor Moriarty, but Conan Doyle doesn't bother to characterize him in the way that, say, Dickens would have done. Who could write more than a brief sentence on the various suspects in *The Hound of the Baskervilles*? They are sufficiently involving while we read, but they have no existence outside the puzzle which has called them into existence.

In fact, one could argue that, far from being her greatest deficiency, it is her characterization that gives Agatha Christie greater universality than all her rivals. If we go to her books looking for psychological depth, complex motivation, the exploration of unusual emotional states, we should at least be clear that we are looking for things that would not for a moment explain her mass popularity. And of course as a rule Agatha Christie provides none of these things. Almost all the well-known crime writers of her generation are "better" than she, judged by such criteria. If we are talking to a Christie enthusiast about, say, *Peril at End House* he may say, "Oh, that's the one that starts off with Poirot deciding that someone is trying to murder a girl, whereas in fact. . . ." In other words, it is the puzzle and its solution that he is likely to remember, the strategy Christie has used to deceive the reader. If the conversation goes beyond this and we start to talk about the other characters in the book, the chances are we neither of us will remember a single one. With Ngaio Marsh or Margery Allingham the reverse would apply. If we talk about *Opening Night* it is the theater milieu we will remember, and the young girl getting her first break on the West End stage. Or if we talk about *More Work for the Undertaker* we will remember the setting of Bloomsbury in decay and the family of eccentric individuals around whom the story revolves. But the chances are in both cases that we will have forgotten who did the murder.

And the vivid characterization and scene-setting of Allingham, wonderfully evocative though they are for readers of a certain British sociointellectual group, work against her as a popular

writer. Bloomsbury, with its very special associations and particular atmosphere, means very little to the average lower-middle or
working-class reader. By being so specific in her settings, by
dwelling lovingly on the typical eccentricities of her characters,
she loses universality.

Now the interesting thing about Agatha Christie is not only that
she uses stereotypes for most or all of her suspects, but that her
stereotypes are not even particularly vivid. There is a sort of general "feel" about her characters: anyone attending Anglican service in a rural community will recognise "Christie characters" in
the sparse and shivering congregation around him. But they have
very little individual coloring or specificity: one cannot distinguish
between Major Burnaby, Major Horton, Major Porter and Major
Palgrave. In fact, what she provides is a sort of basic outline, a bare
minimum. She says, in effect: here is the outline shape of an
Anglo-Indian, or a country squire, or a rural clergyman; fill in the
details for yourself.

The same is true of her settings: there are many who depict the
English village with more vividness and charm than Christie, but
it is Christie who comes to people's minds when they think of the
English village murder mystery. And it is the fact that she is not
aiming at particularity, that her scene painting and characterization are marked by generality rather than vividness, that is her
strength rather than her weakness, precisely this that gives her her
universality. Her books are like a child's coloring-book, where the
basic shape of the picture is provided, and the child fills in the
details and decides on the colors himself.

I believe that the secret of Christie's worldwide appeal is that
the Norwegian teenager and the middle-aged matron whom I
mentioned in my first chapter, who know nothing of Anglo-Indian
colonels or Church of England clergyman and who do not have
them rendered vivid for them by the author, nevertheless manage
to fill in the outline provided for them. And they do this with
details drawn from *their own experience.* Thus, for example, the Italian

lady relates the Anglo-Indian colonel to elderly Italian military men, veteran bores of the Albanian fiasco nostalgic for the age of Mussolini. The Norwegian girl can translate the Anglican clergy-man into the subtly different Lutheran equivalent in communities she is familiar with. They can do this with Christie; they could not do it with Margery Allingham's Bloomsburyites because they are so particular and peculiar, and they are given such a special fictional life.

Thus, as I see it, Agatha Christie only seems to create a vision of England and English society; in fact she creates a broad, rather anonymous society on to which the reader can superimpose his own community, the human types that he himself is familiar with. Just as her characters gain universality *because* they have little psy-chological depth, *because* they are not vivid and particular, so also with the settings: because she cannot (or perhaps we should say, remembering the best of the Mary Westmacott novels, because she does not bother to) write well, Christie never creates any very evocative image of any particular place. One house or one village in her books is very like another. Even when the house is impor-tant (as for example in the posthumous *Sleeping Murder*) she avoids language with emotional overtones and gives it little or no ar-chitectural particularity. And because of this the reader supplies the details for himself, drawn from the houses or the communities he himself knows. My Norwegian teenager thinks she is reading about an English village, but what is really in her mind is an Anglo-Norwegian hybrid village, situated on a fjord somewhere near Torquay.

What I am trying to say about the reasons for Christie's univer-sality is encapsulated in my own mind by an American paperback edition I own of *At Bertram's Hotel*. The cover depicts Miss Marple —a Miss Marple who is a well-preserved lady of a certain age, crowned with a magnificently coiffured head of blue-rinsed hair. But any outrage or amusement one might feel on the subject (and Agatha Christie would probably have felt the former) is tempered by the thought that if this is not how Christie imagined Miss Marple, it is certainly the way she is seen by the average American reader. He has recreated Miss Marple in a transatlantic mold.

The superb plotting and the adequate yet anonymous characterization go a long way to accounting for Agatha Christie's supremacy above all other twentieth-century detective-story writers. Something needs to be said too about her relation to the subject matter of her books—crime. I have suggested already that she took a conventional law-and-order approach, believed emphatically in punishment even unto hanging, and occasionally winked her steel-gray eyes at people who took the law into their own hands. But so far nothing has been said about the treatment of violence in her books, and this seems to me rather special. In *An Autobiography* she states unequivocally that when she began reading and writing detective stories she saw them as morality tales—"the hunting down of Evil and the triumph of Good"—and that for that reason she was shocked by the rather equivocal figure of Raffles (whom she seems to see, wrongly, as standing alone in the early detective story in his ambiguous relationship with the law):

> But Raffles was a light-hearted exception. No one could have dreamt then that there would come a time when crime books would be read for their love of violence, the taking of sadistic pleasure in brutality for its own sake. One would have thought the community would rise up in horror against such things; but now cruelty seems almost everyday bread and butter.

More than one reviewer at the time of publication (including Maurice Richardson in the *Observer*) suggested that Christie displays here a great lack of self-knowledge, and a naïve ignorance of why her books sell: after all, they were almost all about violent death, and they obviously appealed to the sadistic side of a public which delighted in tales of bloodshed and horror.

On the face of it Richardson and the others were undoubtedly right: with so many murders to her credit, many of them very bloody indeed, it must have seemed like gross hypocrisy, or at the very least self-deception, to complain about writers who take "sadistic pleasure in brutality for its own sake." And yet, on reflection, I think Agatha Christie was in the right, and many of the conventional explanations of the appeal of the English style of detective story wrong. That appeal is often described as that of "violence domesticated": people love the fact that these books bring the bloody events they usually only read about in the Sunday papers into the intimacy of their own sitting rooms—the appeal of "the body in the library," in fact.

But the more one reads of these books, and particularly the more one reads of Agatha Christie, the less such an explanation satisfies. Yes—no doubt the addict does like to have murder brought home to him, but not for any sadistic gloating over violence brought thrillingly close. What emotion does the average Christie reader feel when that body is discovered on the library floor? Shock? Horror? Goose pimples around the nape of the neck? No. The primary reaction is surely along the lines of: "Right, here's the body. How is it lying? How long has it been dead? Are the windows open?" and so on. The violence in Christie arouses only the very mildest of frissons; the principal reaction is always intellectual and ratiocinative. None of her books aims at the sort of excitement Conan Doyle achieves in *The Hound of the Baskervilles* or *The Sign of Four:* due to the mode of presentation the violence does not shock or terrify. That Christie capitalizes on the public's interest in crime no one would deny, but it is not the sexual or sadistic interest aroused by, say, the deeds of a Jack the Ripper or her namesake Christie. It is the sort of interest that likes to speculate on exactly how Charles Bravo met his death, on whether conceivably Madeline Smith was innocent, or, for that matter, who it was who killed the Princes in the Tower. The interest in crime she appeals to is not an emotional and sensational one; it is a *curiosity*—the desire to examine the available facts and reason through from them to a convincing solution.

In fact, the sort of story Christie writes is the *only* popular form whose appeal is primarily to the mind, the faculty of reason, rather than to the emotions. Where the thriller invites emotional identification with the hero in his struggle against the forces of darkness, the most the detective form invites is a sort of participation in the continuing process of detection. The reader is a part of the investigative process, matching his wits against both criminal and detective. As John Ritchie says (in his excellent article "Agatha Christie's England 1918–1939"), her appeal "was essentially to the intellect, to the higher parts, divorced from the emotions and the sexual holts, in contrast to the Bond stories of the 'fifties and 'sixties."

Of course, it may be objected that this appeal is on the lowest possible level: that her murders are as unlike any real murder that ever was committed as it is possible to be, and that the process of reasoning that takes place as a consequence is quite worthless, unrelated to any exercise of reason that might take place in everyday life, and therefore existing in a vacuum. But this is to ignore the fact that any popular form has to be granted its conventions: to enjoy James Bond we have to accept his world of pseudo-scientific, death-dealing gadgetry; to enjoy Daphne Du Maurier's *Frenchman's Creek* we have to suspend our skepticism about romantic French pirates; to enjoy a classic Western (alas, realism has invaded that genre too of late) we have to suspend our suspicions about the *real* nature of the men and women who pushed the frontier westward.

Grant the conventions of the detective story, which are no more absurd than those governing any other popular genre, and one ought to respect it as appealing primarily to a human instinct to reason through, to form a total picture from fragmented pieces, to use the brain to bring order from chaos and light from darkness. In fact, Agatha Christie—far from deceiving herself about the place of violence in her books—deserves great credit for shunning the cheaper sorts of titillation and, especially in her classic phase, for conceiving a series of superb puzzles, thought through with great intellectual rigor and put before the reader with scrupulous fairness. Much of the average reader's affection for Christie (a feeling she certainly arouses, even though, with her hatred and distrust of publicity, she did nothing extra-literary to stimulate it) springs from the fact that, within the limitations of this particular popular form, she appealed to his mind, and treated it with respect.

And this unique appeal to the mind is why—however often the funeral service is read over it—the classic whodunnit will never die. Even now, as was suggested earlier, it probably has more *readers* than any other popular form. As far as younger writers are concerned it may well be that it was killed not by any inherent artificiality, not because it ran out of variations, but by its acquired snobbery, which the new generation found repulsive and irrelevant to the world they wanted to depict. When they realize that the formula is infinitely adaptable, can flourish in any setting, with characters of any class or race, can make a genuine comment on the social and moral condition of the world today, then the whodunnit may return in force—perhaps has already begun to do so. It is worth noting that some of the more recent practitioners of the California school, for example, the much-praised Brown Meggs, superimpose a relentlessly realistic style of characterization and setting on to distinctly Christiean tricks of plotting. He is not the only one to find that the formula is infinitely adaptable, as well as being, for most readers, marvelously entertaining.

It was Christie's great strength that she never forgot that she was an entertainer, never pretended to be anything other than a popular writer. Jacques Barzun's complaint that with its new realism, psychological and social, the detective story has "ceased to give entertainment" may be an exaggeration, but it contains the seeds of truth, and constitutes a terrible warning. Christie was, by his definition, a teller of tales, and content to remain so. It was distrusting the value of tales that led Dorothy L. Sayers from being a writer of lively detective stories to being a writer of mediocre middle-brow novels. However much Lord Peter may irritate, however much the racial and social attitudes may repel, one cannot deny that *Clouds of Witness* and *The Unpleasantness at the Bellona Club* are highly entertaining stories, with some wonderfully tricky detection. Who in their senses would exchange them for the longueurs of *Have His Carcase* or *Gaudy Night?* And because of her prestige and her evangelist instincts Sayers spread the disease well beyond her own work: several Allingham books of the late 'thirties (for example, *The Fashion in Shrouds*) became allusive and pretentious precisely by aiming to be that most shiver-making thing "a respectable form of literature." Josephine Tey also squirmed with the detective formula (had she not written dull historical plays?) and began producing entertaining novelettes with a mildly detective flavor. From all such ambitions Agatha Christie was blessedly free. She always knew what she was: "one is a tradesman —a tradesman in a good honest trade."

And if she had no desire to elevate her "trade" into a "profession" by writing anything that could be confused with a "real novel," still less was she bitten by the fine-writing bug. Her own estimate of her capacities in that direction has been quoted, and it is modest but not unfair. She could write competently—she certainly might without detriment have taken a little more care. But her good sense saved her from the sort of ambitions nourished by her foremost rival: just as Sayers's idea of making the detective story intellectually respectable was to have her characters fling around quotations as if they were Ping-Pong balls, so her idea of literary style was a pretentious and convoluted mishmash, like George Eliot in gumboots. The main characteristic of Agatha Christie's writing is that one does not notice it. And that, perhaps, is about the highest praise one could give to a writer of popular literature.

In fact, all the common grounds of criticism and ridicule used against Agatha Christie work with a boomerang effect when we realize that she was essentially, and aimed to be, a popular writer, a good teller of tales. Her drab style is admirably suited to such an aim. We do not go to popular literature for fine writing, we go to it for relief from fine writing. Our main requirement is that the author gets on with the story and doesn't allow anything to interfere with the narrative flow, and this she invariably does. Similarly with characterization and setting, as we have seen: in the tale they must be subordinate to the incidents; they must support them but not obtrude themselves into too independent an existence. By never luxuriating in her exotic settings, or sentimentalizing her English ones; by never letting any one character loom too large (if he does, like Mrs. Boynton, we can be sure he will soon be removed) or monopolize interest by too great a psychological complexity, she places the interest fair and square where in popular literature it belongs—in the narration of events.

All her supposed weaknesses are thus part of her strength as a popular writer. And the beauty of that narrative which she places at the forefront of the interest, and plans so meticulously, is that, like a bud opening into flower, we have a sense of initial mystery and concealment which gradually unfolds to reveal a design of patterned intricacy and beauty. And by this progression from meaningful mystery to enlightenment, the pattern of all her best books, she mirrors every reader's experience of life around him— the deceiving surfaces of it, the façades other people put up before their neighbor's inquiring gaze, which gradually come down and give way to a deeper knowledge of the passions that drive them. Her books are the literary equivalent of that most universal human curiosity, the desire to penetrate the secrets of our fellow humans' lives.

What will be the fate of her books in the next fifty, the next hundred years is anybody's guess. One thing we can be sure of: those who regard the Sherlock Holmes societies and reenactments of the famous fatality at the Reichenbach Falls as a species of the higher lunacy we can well do without can surely rest assured that no similar cult will embrace Poirot, Hastings, George and Miss

Lemon. They lack the recognizable humanity of Holmes and Watson, and the densely imagined physical environment as well. They do not have sufficient independence as creations to affect people's imaginations in that way. And could one, today, find a St. Mary Mead to build a cult around?

But that the English detective stories of the Golden Age can take hold of people's imaginations in a quite other way is evidenced by the multitude of recent parodies I mentioned earlier. Joe Orton and his friend Kenneth Halliwell went to jail for defacing, among other books, a Peter Wimsey novel with a cod blurb promising all sorts of indecent surprises in the course of the noble lord's investigations. But when he came to write *Loot* Orton sent up the conventions of the classical detective story in a way that was not only hilarious, but also affectionate. The stuff of the whodunnit became the material for many un-Christiean reflections on the nature of British law and justice, but it also was transformed into fantastical farce of a truly Wildean delicacy and wit. I doubt whether this could have happened if the material Orton was parodying did not have in itself a literary vitality of some sort, and did not genuinely answer some human craving.

One is reminded of the fashion in the early nineteenth century for writing sendups of the popular "Gothic" novels: parodies of one kind or another were written by Peacock, Byron, Jane Austen, and others, and most of these parodies suggest that the ridicule was inspired by affection rather than contempt. The strength of *Northanger Abbey* lies not only in the fact that it hilariously parodies a form that was ripe for ridicule; as many critics have pointed out, it is effective because Jane Austen acknowledges the force of the Gothic novel's appeal to one side of herself—an emotional, sensation-craving side that she usually found it necessary to suppress in her writing. The same is true of Orton and the other modern parodists of the detective story: while they ridicule its artificiality and snobbery, they acknowledge the appeal it makes to sides of their nature which it is unfashionable to indulge—a love of order, certainty, rationality.

And it may be that, just as—in spite of the ridicule of the intellectuals of the time—the Gothic novel still maintains a toe-hold in English literature, continues to be read by devotees and even recreated by a Daphne du Maurier, so perhaps the detective story of the classic British type will maintain a similar fringe literary existence, never quite accepted or respectable yet not entirely cast out on to the garbage heaps of forgotten literary fashion —a Duchess of Windsor sort of existence, never quite in and never quite out.

Certain it is that Agatha Christie's durability is already astonishing, and shows no sign of waning. Ian Fleming has been dead only fifteen years, but already one can see signs that Bond has peaked and is in decline, needing badly the hormone injections of those bad films. Roger Ackroyd was murdered more than fifty years ago, yet there are still as many people as ever who care who killed him. The irritation one felt at the garrulity and the slackened grip of those last Christie novels cannot alter the fact that Christmas has not felt the same these last few years without her offering. Already the signs are that she will not suffer seriously from the slump in reputation that most writers experience after their death. So already we are beginning to get the idea that as well as spanning age, intelligence and class barriers she will jump the gap that separates her era from succeeding ones.

Why? She created a timeless, changeless world, peopled by cardboard characters who somehow manage to maintain our interest in that dazzling conjuring trick that is to be performed on page 190. She nourished our instinctive hopes that in the end right and truth will triumph over the evil and the obscure. And she brought murder into the home, where it belonged, seeing the murderous glint in the eye of the self-effacing bank clerk, the homicidal madness in the flutterings of the genteel lady companion. Chandler saw evil in the social organisms of which we are part; Christie saw it in our wives, our friends, the quiet circle of which we are a part. And perhaps thereby she made us sense it in ourselves.

APPENDICES

I
Bibliography
(compiled by Louise
Barnard)

THE ABC MURDERS:
>London: Collins, 1936. 252 pp.
>New York: Dodd, Mead & Co., 1936, 306 pp.
>New York: Pocket Books, 1941. (PB)
>Harmondsworth: Penguin, 1948. 224 pp. (PB)
>London: Pan, 1958. 191 pp. (PB)
>London: Fontana, 1972. 192 pp. (PB)
>London: Collins, 1976 (Greenway edition) 251 pp.
>New York: Pocket Books, 1976. (PB)
>New York: Dodd, Mead & Co., 1978 (Greenway edition). 251 pp.
>London: Pan, 1979. 191 pp. (PB)
>See also omnibus editions: *Murder-Go-Round; Surprise Endings by Hercule Poirot.*

ABSENT IN THE SPRING (Mary Westmacott, pseudonym):
>London: Collins, 1944. 160 pp.
>New York: Farrar & Rinehart, 1944. 250 pp.

New York: Dell, 1967. 192 pp. (PB)
New York: Arbor House, 1971. 250 pp.
London: Collins, 1973. 192 pp.
London: Fontana, 1974. 192 pp.

THE ADVENTURE OF THE CHRISTMAS PUDDING AND A SELECTION OF ENTREES
(short-story collection):
London: Collins, 1960. 255 pp.
London: Fontana, 1963. 224 pp. (PB)

AFTER THE FUNERAL:
London: Collins, 1953. 191 pp.
London: Fontana, 1956. 191 pp. (PB)
Leicester, Eng.: Ulverscroft Large Print Edition, 1968. 237 pp.
Leicester, Eng.: Ulverscroft Large Print Edition, 1978. 422 pp.
See also omnibus edition: *A Poirot Quintet.*

—with United States title: FUNERALS ARE FATAL:
New York: Dodd, Mead & Co., 1953. 244 pp.
New York: Pocket Books, 194. 224 pp. (PB)
See also omnibus edition: *Murder-Go-Round.*

AFTERNOON AT THE SEASIDE. A PLAY IN ONE ACT:
London: French, 1963. 35 pp.

AGATHA CHRISTIE. AN AUTOBIOGRAPHY
see *An Autobiography.*

THE AGATHA CHRISTIE HOUR (short stories which formed the basis of a
television series, drawn from *The Hound of Death, The Listerdale
Mystery, Parker Pyne Investigates* and *Miss Marple's Final Cases.* Includes "Magnolia Blossom", for the first time in the U.K. in volume
form):
London: Collins, 1982, 190 pp.

AN AGATHA CHRISTIE OMNIBUS (contents: The Mysterious Affair at Styles;
Murder on the Links; Poirot Investigates):
London: John Lane, 1931.

THE AGATHA CHRISTIE OMNIBUS OF CRIME (contents: The Sittaford Mystery; The Seven Dials Mystery; The Mystery of the Blue Train; The Murder of Roger Ackroyd):
London: Collins, 1932. Separate pagination.

AGATHA CHRISTIE'S CRIME READER (contents: Selections from Poirot Investigates; The Mysterious Mr Quin; Partners in Crime):
Cleveland: World Publishing Co., 1944. Separate pagination.

AKHNATON. A PLAY IN THREE ACTS:
London: Collins, 1973. 157 pp.
New York: Dodd, Mead & Co., 1973. 157 pp.

ALIBI (dramatization by Michael Morton of The Murder of Roger Ackroyd):
London: French, 1929.

AND THEN THERE WERE NONE
see Ten Little Niggers.

APPOINTMENT WITH DEATH:
London: Collins, 1938. 252 pp.
New York: Dodd, Mead & Co., 1938. 301 pp.
New York: Dell, 1946. 192 pp. (PB)
Harmondsworth: Penguin, 1948. 206 pp. (PB)
London: Pan, 1957. 159 pp. (PB)
London: Fontana, 1960. 159 pp. (PB)
Leicester, Eng.: Ulverscroft Large Print Edition, 1975. 334 pp.
See also omnibus edition: Make Mine Murder.

APPOINTMENT WITH DEATH. A PLAY IN THREE ACTS:
London: French, 1956. 76 pp.
See also The Mousetrap and Other Plays.

AT BERTRAM'S HOTEL:
London: Collins, 1965. 255 pp.
New York: Dodd, Mead & Co., 1966. 272 pp.
New York: Pocket Books, 1967. 180 pp. (PB)
London: fontana, 1968. 192 pp. (PB)
Leicester, Eng.: Ulverscroft Large Print Edition, 1968. 256 pp.

London: Collins, 1972 (Greenway edition). 253 pp.
New York: Dodd, Mead & Co., 1973 (Greenway edition). 253 pp.
See also omnibus edition: *A Miss Marple Quintet.*

AN AUTOBIOGRAPHY:

London: Collins, 1977. 542 pp., illus.
New York: Dodd, Mead & Co., 1977. 529 pp., illus.
London: Fontana, 1978. 576 pp., illus. (PB)
Leicester, Eng.: Ulverscroft Large Print Edition, 2 vols., 1979. Vol. 1,
    611 pp.; vol. 2, 535 pp.

THE BIG FOUR:

London: Collins, 1927. 281 pp.
New York: Dodd, Mead & Co., 1927. 276 pp.
New York: Avon, 1941 (PB)
Harmondsworth: Penguin, 1957. 159 pp. (PB)
London: Pan, 1961. 155 pp. (PB)
London: Fontana, 1965. 159 pp. (PB)
New York: Dell, 1965. 173 pp. (PB)
Leicester, Eng.: Ulverscroft Large Print Edition, 1974. 312 pp.

BLACK COFFEE. A PLAY IN THREE ACTS:
London: A. Ashley, 1934. 75 pp.
London: French, 1952. 70 pp.

THE BODY IN THE LIBRARY:

London: Collins, 1942. 160 pp.
New York: Dodd, Mead & Co., 1942. 245 pp.
New York: Pocket Books, 1946. 152 pp. (PB)
Harmondsworth: Penguin, 1953. 190 pp. (PB)
London: Pan, 1959. 157 pp. (PB)
London: Fontana, 1962. 191 pp. (PB)
Leicester, Eng.: Ulverscroft Large Print Edition, 1972. 305 pp.
See also omnibus editions: *Murder in Our Midst; Starring Miss Marple.*

THE BOOMERANG CLUE

see *Why Didn't They Ask Evans?*

THE BURDEN (Mary Westmacott, pseudonym):
London: Heinemann, 1956. 236 pp.
New York: Dell, 1963. 223 pp. (PB)

London: Collins, 1973. 192 pp.
New York: Arbor House, 1973. 223 pp.
London: Fontana, 1975. 192 pp. (PB)
Leicester, Eng.: Ulverscroft Large Print Edition, 1979. 321 pp.

BY THE PRICKING OF MY THUMBS:

London: Collins, 1968. 255 pp.
New York: Dodd, Mead & Co., 1968. 275 pp.
New York: Pocket Books, 1969. 208 pp. (PB)
London: Fontana, 1971. 191 pp. (PB)

CARDS ON THE TABLE:

London: Collins, 1936. 286 pp.
New York: Dodd, Mead & Co., 1937. 262 pp.
New York: Dodd, Mead & Co., 1949. 190 pp. (PB)
London: Pan, 1951. 186 pp. (PB)
London: Fontana, 1957. 192 pp. (PB)
London: Collins, 1968 (Greenway edition). 253 pp.
New York: Dodd, Mead & Co., 1968 (Greenway edition). 253 pp.
Leicester, Eng.: Ulverscroft Large Print Edition, 1969. 343 pp.
See also omnibus edition: *Surprise Endings by Hercule Poirot.*

A CARIBBEAN MYSTERY:

London: Collins, 1964. 256 pp.
New York: Dodd, Mead & Co., 1965. 245 pp.
London: Fontana, 1966. 157 pp. (PB)
New York: Pocket Books, 1966. 176 pp. (PB)
Leicester, Eng.: Ulverscroft Large Print Books, 1966. 194 pp.
New York: Dodd, Mead & Co., 1979 (Greenway Edition). 256 pp.

CAT AMONG THE PIGEONS:

London: Collins, 1959. 255 pp.
New York: Dodd, Mead & Co., 1960. 224 pp.
New York: Pocket Books, 1961. 216 pp. (PB)
London: Fontana, 1962. 187 pp. (PB)
Leicester, Eng.: Ulverscroft Large Print Edition, 1964. 255 pp.

CHRISTIE CLASSICS (contents: The Murder of Roger Ackroyd; And Then There
    Were None; "The Witness for the Prosecution"; "Philomel Cot-
    tage"; "Three Blind Mice"):

New York: Dodd, Mead & Co., 1957. 410 pp.

THE CLOCKS:

London: Collins, 1963. 256 pp.
New York: Dodd, Mead & Co., 1964. 276 pp.
New York: Pocket Books, 1965. 246 pp.
London: Fontana, 1966. 221 pp. (PB)
Leicester, Eng.: Ulverscroft Large Print Edition, 1969. 417 pp.

COME, TELL ME HOW YOU LIVE (nondetective):

London: Collins, 1946. 192 pp.
New York: Dodd, Mead & Co., 1946. 225 pp.
London: Collins, 1976. Rev. ed. 192 pp., illus.
New York: Dodd, Mead & Co., 1976. 192 pp.
New York: Pocket Books, 1977. 222 pp. (PB)
London: The Bodley Head, 1983, with a new introduction by Jacquetta
    Hawkes, 192 pp.

THE CRIME READER

see *Agatha Christie's Crime Reader.*

CROOKED HOUSE:

London: Collins, 1949. 192 pp.
New York: Dodd, Mead & Co., 1949. 211 pp.
New York: Pocket Books, 1951. 200 pp. (PB)
Harmondsworth: Penguin, 1953. 191 pp. (PB)
London: Fontana, 1959. 191 pp. (PB)
London: Collins, 1967 (Greenway edition). 223 pp.
New York: Dodd, Mead & Co., 1967 (Greenway edition). 223 pp.
See also omnibus edition: *The Nursery Rhyme Murders.*

CURTAIN:

London: Collins, 1975. 221 pp.
New York: Dodd, Mead & Co., 1975. 238 pp.
New York: Pocket Books, 1976. 280 pp. (PB)
Leicester, Eng.: Ulverscroft Large Print Edition, 1976. 325 pp.
London: Fontana, 1977. 188 pp. (PB)

A DAUGHTER'S A DAUGHTER (Mary Westmacott, pseudonym):

London: Heinemann, 1952. 200 pp.
New York: Dell, 1963. 191 pp. (PB)
New York: Arbor House, 1972. 191 pp.

DEAD MAN'S FOLLY:

London: Collins, 1956. 256 pp.
New York: Dodd, Mead & Co., 1956. 216 pp.
New York: Pocket Books, 1957. 178 pp. (PB)
London: Fontana, 1960. 192 pp. (PB)
London: Pan, 1966. 189 pp. (PB)
Leicester, Eng.: Ulverscroft Large Print Edition, 1967. 205 pp.
London: Fontana, 1970. 192 pp.

DEAD MAN'S MIRROR AND OTHER STORIES (substantially the same as Murder in the Mews):

New York: Dodd, Mead & Co., 1937. 290 pp.
New York: Dell, 1958. 190 pp. (PB)

DEATH COMES AS THE END:

New York: Dodd, Mead & Co., 1944. 223 pp.
London: Collins, 1945. 159 pp.
New York: Pocket Books, 1947. 179 pp. (PB)
Harmondsworth: Penguin, 1953. 188 pp. (PB)
London: Fontana, 1960. 191 pp. (PB)
London: Pan, 1963. 221 pp. (PB)
Leicester, Eng.: Ulverscroft Large Print Edition, 1970. 352 pp.
London: Fontana, 1970. 191 pp. (PB)
See also omnibus edition: *Murder International.*

DEATH IN THE AIR

see *Death in the Clouds.*

DEATH IN THE CLOUDS:

London: Collins, 1935. 252 pp.
London: Fontana, 1957. 188 pp. (PB)
London: Pan, 1964. 188 pp. (PB)
Leicester, Eng.: Ulverscroft Large Print Edition, 1967. 219 pp.
London: Collins, 1973 (Greenway edition). 256 pp.
New York: Dodd, Mead & Co., 1974 (Greenway edition). 256 pp.

—with United States title: DEATH IN THE AIR:

New York: Dodd, Mead & Co., 1935. 304 pp.
New York: Avon Book Co, 1946. 259 pp. (PB)
New York: Popular Library, 1961. 189 pp. (PB)
See also omnibus edition: *Murder on Board.*

DEATH ON THE NILE:

London: Collins, 1937. 284 pp.
New York: Dodd, Mead & Co., 1938. 327 pp.
New York: Avon Book Co., 1944. 272 pp. (PB)
London: Pan, 1949. 255 pp. (PB)
Harmondsworth: Penguin, 1953. 249 pp. (PB)
London: Fontana, 1960. 253 pp. (PB)
New York: Bantam, 1963. 214 pp. (PB)
London: Collins, 1969 (Greenway edition). 318 pp.
New York: Dodd, Mead & Co., 1970 (Greenway edition). 318 pp.
Leicester, Eng.: Ulverscroft Large Print Edition, 1971. 466 pp.
London: Collins, 1978 (film edition). 320 pp.
See also omnibus editions: *Perilous Journeys of Hercule Poirot; Masterpieces of Murder; A Poirot Quintet.*

DESTINATION UNKNOWN:

London: Collins, 1954. 191 pp.
London: Fontana, 1958. 191 pp. (PB)
Leicester, Eng.: Ulverscroft Large Print Edition, 1969. 203 pp.
London: Collins, 1977 (Greenway edition). 196 pp.
New York: Dodd, Mead & Co., 1978 (Greenway edition). 196 pp.

—with United States title: SO MANY STEPS TO DEATH:

New York: Dodd, Mead & Co., 1955. 212 pp.
New York: Pocket Books, 1956. 183 pp. (PB)
See also omnibus edition: *Murder International.*

DOUBLE SIN AND OTHER STORIES:

New York: Dodd, Mead & Co., 1961. 247 pp.
New York: Pocket books, 1962. 181 pp. (PB)
New York: Dell, 1964. 191 pp. (PB)

DUMB WITNESS:

London: Collins, 1937. 316 pp.
London: Pan, 1949. 250 pp. (PB)
London: Fontana, 1958. 255 pp. (PB)
London: Pan, 1969. 218 pp. (PB)
Leicester, Eng.: Ulverscroft Large Print Edition, 1973. 454 pp.
London: Fontana, 1975. 255 pp. (PB)
See also omnibus edition: *A Poirot Quintet.*

—with United States title: POIROT LOSES A CLIENT:

New York: Dodd, Mead & Co., 1937. 302 pp.
New York: Avon Book Co., 1945. 260 pp. (PB)
New York: Dell, 1965. 252 pp. (PB)

EASY TO KILL

see *Murder Is Easy.*

ELEPHANTS CAN REMEMBER:

London: Collins, 1972. 256 pp.
New York: Dodd, Mead & Co., 1972. 243 pp.
New York: Dell, 1973. 237 pp. (PB)
New York: G. K. Hall, 1973 (Large Print Books). 362 pp.
London: Fontana, 1975. 160 pp. (PB)
London: Collins, 1978 (Greenway edition). 256 pp.
New York: Dodd, Mead & Co., 1979 (Greenway edition). 256 pp.

ENDLESS NIGHT:

London: Collins, 1967. 224 pp.
New York: Dodd, Mead & Co., 1968. 248 pp.
New York: Pocket Books, 1969. 181 pp. (PB)
London: Fontana, 1970. 192 pp. (PB)
Leicester: Ulverscroft Large Print Edition, 1972. 342 pp.

EVIL UNDER THE SUN:

London: Collins, 1941. 252 pp.
New York: Dodd, Mead & Co., 1941. 260 pp.
New York: Pocket Books, 1945. 183 pp. (PB)
London: Fontana, 1957. 189 pp. (PB)
London: Pan, 1963. 217 pp. (PB)
Leicester: Ulverscroft Large Print Edition, 1971. 362 pp.
London: Fontana, 1977. 189 pp. (PB)
See also omnibus edition: *Murder International.*

EYE WITNESS TO MURDER

(serial title of *4.50 From Paddington*).

FIVE LITTLE PIGS:

London: Collins, 1942. 192 pp.
London: Pan, 1953. 189 pp. (PB)
London: Fontana, 1959. 192 pp. (PB)

—with United States title: MURDER IN RETROSPECT:
New York: Dodd, Mead & Co., 1942. 234 pp.
New York: Dell, 1948. 192 pp. (PB)
See also omnibus edition: *Murder Preferred.*

THE FLOATING ADMIRAL (composite novel by "Certain Members of the
Detection Club", including Christie, Dorothy L. Sayers, G.K.
Chesterton, etc.):
London: Hodder and Stoughton, 1931.
New York: Doubleday, 1931.
New York: Charter Books, 1980, 309 pp.
London: Hamlyn, 1983, 224 pp.

4.50 FROM PADDINGTON:
London: Fontana, 1950. 190 pp. (PB)
London: Collins, 1957. 256 pp.
Leicester, Ulverscroft Large Print Edition, 1965. 256 pp.
London: Pan, 1974. 220 pp. (PB)

—with United States title: MURDER SHE SAID:
New York: Pocket Books, 1961. 211 pp. (PB)

—with United States title: WHAT MRS. MCGILLICUDDY SAW!:
New York: Dodd, Mead & Co., 1957. 192 pp.
New York: Pocket Books, 1958. 185 pp. (PB)
See also omnibus edition: *Murder on Board.*

FUNERALS ARE FATAL
see *After the Funeral.*

GIANT'S BREAD (Mary Westmacott, pseudonym):
London: Collins, 1930. 437 pp.
New York: Doubleday, 1930. 358 pp.
New York: Dell, 1964. 320 pp. (PB)
London: Collins, 1973. 350 pp.
New York: Arbor House, 1973. 312 pp.
London: Fontana, 1975. 288 pp. (PB)
Leicester, Eng.: Ulverscroft Large Print Edition, 1980. 577 pp.

Go Back for Murder. A Play (dramatization of *Five Little Pigs*):
London: French, 1960. 81 pp.
See also: *The Mousetrap and Other Plays.*

The Golden Ball and Other Stories (contains most of the stories from *The Listerdale Mystery* and *The Hound of Death*):
New York: Dodd, Mead & Co., 1971. 280 pp.
New York: Dell, 1972. 235 pp. (PB)

Hallowe'en Party:
London: Collins, 1969. 255 pp.
New York: Dodd, Mead & Co., 1969. 248 pp.
New York: Pocket Books, 1970. 185 pp. (PB)
London: Fontana, 1972. 189 pp. (PB)

Hercule Poirot: Master Detective (contents: The Murder of Roger Ackroyd; Murder in the Calais Coach; Thirteen at Dinner):
New York: Dodd, Mead & Co., 1936. Separate pagination.

Hercule Poirot's Christmas:
London: Collins, 1938. 251 pp.
London: Fontana, 1957. 189 pp. (PB)
London: Pan, 1967. 204 pp. (PB)
London: Fontana, 1972. 189 pp. (PB)
London: Collins, 1973 (Greenway edition). 253 pp.
New York: Dodd, Mead & Co., 1974 (Greenway edition). 253 pp.

—with United States title: A Holiday for Murder:
New York: Avon Book Co., 1947. 255 pp. (PB)
New York: Bantam, 1962. 167 pp. (PB)

—with United States title: Murder for Christmas:
New York: Dodd, Mead & Co., 1939. 272 pp.

Hercule Poirot's Early Cases
see *Poirot's Early Cases.*

Hickory, Dickory Death
see *Hickory, Dickory Dock.*

HICKORY, DICKORY DOCK:
    London: Collins, 1955. 191 pp.
    London: Fontana, 1958. 192 pp. (PB)
    London: Pan, 1967. 189 pp. (PB)
    London: Fontana, 1972. 192 pp. (PB)

—with United States title: HICKORY, DICKORY DEATH:
    New York: Dodd, Mead & Co., 1955. 241 pp.
    New York: Pocket Books, 1956. 152 pp. (PB)
    See also omnibus edition: *The Nursery Rhyme Murders.*

A HOLIDAY FOR MURDER
    see *Hercule Poirot's Christmas.*

THE HOLLOW:
    London: Collins, 1946. 256 pp.
    New York: Dodd, Mead & Co., 1946. 279 pp.
    New York: Pocket Books, 1948 (PB)
    London: Pan, 1950. 239 pp. (PB)
    London: Fontana, 1957. 189 pp. (PB)
    Leicester, Eng.: Ulverscroft Large Print Edition, 1974. 431 pp.
    London: Pan, 1975. 219 pp. (PB)

—with United States title: MURDER AFTER HOURS:
    New York: Dell, 1954. 255 pp. (PB)

THE HOLLOW. A PLAY IN THREE ACTS (dramatization):
    London: French, 1952. 94 pp.
    See also: *The Mousetrap and Other Plays.*

THE HOUND OF DEATH AND OTHER STORIES:
    London: Collins, 1933. 247 pp.
    London: Pan, 1960. 218 pp. (PB)
    London: Fontana, 1964. 190 pp. (PB)
    Leicester, Eng.: Ulverscroft Large Print Edition, 1968. 218 pp.
    Leicester, Eng.: Ulverscroft Large Print Edition, 1978. 375 pp.

THE LABOURS OF HERCULES (short-story collection):
    London: Collins, 1947. 256 pp.
    New York: Dodd, Mead & Co., 1947. 265 pp.

New York: Dell, 1951. 255 pp. (PB)
Harmondsworth: Penguin, 1953. 254 pp. (PB)
London: Fontana, 1961. 256 pp. (PB)
London: Collins, 1967 (Greenway edition). 319 pp.
New York: Dodd, Mead & Co., 1967 (Greenway edition). 319 pp.
Leicester, Eng.: Ulverscroft Large Print Edition, 1978. 467 pp.

THE LISTERDALE MYSTERY (short-story collection):
London: Collins, 1934. 251 pp.
London: Fontana, 1961. 192 pp. (PB)
London: Pan, 1970. 188 pp. (PB)
London: Fontana, 1975. 192 pp. (PB)

LORD EDGWARE DIES:
London: Collins, 1933. 252 pp.
Harmondsworth: Penguin, 1948. 251 pp. (PB)
London: Fontana, 1954. 192 pp. (PB)
London: Collins, 1969 (Greenway edition). 255 pp.
New York: Dodd, Mead & Co., 1970 (Greenway edition). 255 pp.
Leicester, Eng.: Ulverscroft Large Print Edition, 1970. 380 pp.

—with U.S. title: THIRTEEN AT DINNER:
New York: Dodd, Mead & Co., 1933. 305 pp.
New York: Dell, 1944. 224 pp. (PB)
See also omnibus editions: *Hercule Poirot: Master Detective; Murder-Go-Round; Three Christie Crimes.*

LOVE FROM A STRANGER. A PLAY IN THREE ACTS (dramatization by Frank Vosper of "Philomel Cottage"):
London: French, 1937.

MAKE MINE MURDER (contents: Appointment with Death; Peril at End House, Sad Cypress):
New York: Dodd, Mead & Co., 1962. 473 pp.

THE MAN IN THE BROWN SUIT:
London: John Lane, 1924. 310 pp.
New York: Dodd, Mead & Co., 1924. 275 pp.
New York: Dell, 1949. 223 pp. (PB)
London: Pan, 1953. 190 pp. (PB)
London: Panther, 1978. 192 pp. (PB)

MASTERPIECES OF MURDER (contents: The Murder of Roger Ackroyd; And Then There Were None; "The Witness for the Prosecution"; Death on the Nile):
New York: Dodd, Mead & Co., 1977. 594 pp.

THE MIRROR CRACK'D
see *the Mirror Crack'd from Side to Side.*

THE MIRROR CRACK'D FROM SIDE TO SIDE:
London: Collins, 1962. 255 pp.
London: Fontana, 1965. 192 pp. (PB)
Leicester, Eng.: Ulverscroft Large Print Edition, 1966. 255 pp.
Harmondsworth: Penguin, 1974. 224 pp. (PB)
See also omnibus edition: *A Miss Marple Quintet.*

—with U.S. title: THE MIRROR CRACK'D:
New York: Dodd, Mead & Co., 1963. 246 pp.
New York: Pocket Books, 1964.

A MISS MARPLE QUINTET (contents: The Murder at the Vicarage; The Mirror Crack'd from Side to Side; A Murder Is Announced; A Pocket Full of Rye; At Bertram's Hotel):
London: Collins, 1978. 912 pp.

MISS MARPLE'S FINAL CASES (short-story collection):
London: Collins, 1979.

MR. PARKER PYNE, DETECTIVE
see *Parker Pyne Investigates.*

MRS. MCGINTY'S DEAD:
London: Collins, 1952. 187 pp.
New York: Dodd, Mead & Co., 1952. 243 pp.
New York: Pocket Books, 1953. 181 pp. (PB)
London: Fontana, 1957. 188 pp. (PB)
London: Pan, 1970. 191 pp. (PB)
London: Fontana, 1974. 188 pp. (PB)

THE MOUSETRAP. A PLAY IN TWO ACTS (dramatization of "Three Blind Mice"):

London: French, 1954. 70 pp.
See also: *The Mousetrap and Other Plays*.

THE MOUSETRAP (short-story collection)
see *Three Blind Mice and Other Stories*.

THE MOUSETRAP AND OTHER PLAYS (contents: Ten Little Indians; Appointment with Death; The Hollow; The Mousetrap; Witness for the Prosecution; Towards Zero; Verdict; Go Back for Murder):

New York: Dodd, Mead & Co., 1978. 659 pp.

THE MOVING FINGER:

New York: Dodd, Mead & Co., 1942. 229 pp.
London: Collins, 1943. 160 pp.
New York: Avon Book Co., 1948. 158 pp. (PB)
London: Pan, 1948. 190 pp. (PB)
Harmondsworth: Penguin, 1953. 189 pp. (PB)
London: Fontana, 1961. 160 pp. (PB)
New York: Dell, 1964. 189 pp. (PB)
London: Collins, 1968 (Greenway edition). 255 pp.
New York: Dodd, Mead & Co., 1968 (Greenway edition). 255 p.
Leicester, Eng.: Ulverscroft Large Print Edition, 1970. 331 pp.
See also omnibus edition: *Murder in Our Midst*.

MURDER AFTER HOURS
see *The Hollow*.

MURDER AT HAZELMOOR
see *The Sittaford Mystery*.

THE MURDER AT THE VICARAGE:

London: Collins, 1930. 254 pp.
New York: Dodd, Mead & Co., 1930. 319 pp.
Harmondsworth: Penguin, 1948. 255 pp. (PB)
New York: Dell, 1948. 223 pp. (PB)
London: Fontana, 1961. 191 pp. (PB)
London: Collins, 1976 (Greenway edition), 1978. 251 pp.

New York: Dodd, Mead & Co., (Greenway edition). 251 pp.
Leicester Eng.: Ulverscroft Large Print Edition,
See also omnibus editions: *Murder in Our Midst; A Miss Marple Quintet.*

THE MURDER AT THE VICARAGE (dramatization by M. Charles and B. Toy):
London: French, 1950.

MURDER FOR CHRISTMAS
see *Hercule Poirot's Christmas.*

MURDER-GO-ROUND (contents: Thirteen at Dinner; the ABC Murders; Funerals Are Fatal):
New York: Dodd, Mead & Co., 1972. 638 pp.

MURDER IN MESOPOTAMIA:
London: Collins, 1936. 284 pp.
New York: Dodd, Mead & Co., 1936. 298 pp.
New York: Dell, 1944. 223 pp. (PB)
Harmondsworth: Penguin, 1955. 219 pp. (PB)
London: Fontana, 1962. 190 pp. (PB)
Leicester, Eng.: Ulverscroft Large Print Edition, 1969. 367 pp.
see also omnibus editions: *Perilous Journeys of Hercule Poirot; Spies among Us.*

MURDER IN OUR MIDST (contents: The Body in the Library; The Murder at the Vicarage; The Moving Finger):
New York: Dodd, Mead & Co., 1967. 444 pp.

MURDER IN THE CALAIS COACH
see *Murder on the Orient Express.*

MURDER IN THE MEWS AND THREE OTHER POIROT CASES (see also Dead Man's Mirror and Other Stories):
London: Collins, 1937. 280 pp.
London: Fontana, 1958. 190 pp. (PB)
Harmondsworth: Penguin, 1961. 221 pp. (PB)
London: Collins, 1967. 288 pp.
London: Pan, 1976. 189 pp. (PB)

MURDER IN RETROSPECT
see *Five Little Pigs*.

MURDER IN THREE ACTS
see *Three Act Tragedy*.

MURDER INTERNATIONAL (contents: So Many Steps to Death; Death Comes as
the End; Evil under the Sun):
New York: Dodd, Mead & Co., 1965. 478 pp.

A MURDER IS ANNOUNCED:
London: Collins, 1950. 256 pp.
New York: Dodd, Mead & Co., 1950. 248 pp.
New York: Pocket Books, 1951. 229 pp. (PB)
London: Fontana, 1953. 191 pp. (PB)
London: Pan, 1958. 204 pp. (PB)
Leicester, Eng.: Ulverscroft Large Print Edition, 1965. 246 pp.
London: Collins, 1967 (Greenway edition). 288 pp.
New York: Dodd, Mead & Co., 1967 (Greenway edition). 288 pp.
London: Fontana, 1974. 221 pp. (PB)
See also omnibus editions: *Murder Preferred; Starring Miss Marple; A
Miss Marple Quintet*.

A MURDER IS ANNOUNCED (dramatization by L. Darbon):
London: French, 1978. 72 pp.

MURDER IS EASY:

London: Collins, 1939. 254 pp.
London: Pan, 1951. 250 pp. (PB)
Harmondsworth: Penguin, 1957. 172 pp. (PB)
London: Fontana, 1960. 190 pp. (PB)
Leicester, Eng.: Ulverscroft Large Print Edition, 1966. 219 pp.

—with U.S. title: EASY TO KILL:
New York: Dodd, Mead & Co., 1939. 248 pp.
New York: Pocket Books, 1945. 152 pp. (PB)

THE MURDER OF ROGER ACKROYD:

London: Collins, 1926. 312 pp.
New York: Dodd, Mead & Co., 1926. 306 pp.
London: Collins, 1939 (Canterbury Classics). 336 pp., illus.
New York: Pocket Books, 1939. 212 pp. (PB)
Harmondsworth: Penguin, 1948. 250 pp. (PB)
London: Fontana, 1957. 254 pp. (PB)
London: Collins, 1964 (Modern Author Series). 254 pp.
London: Collins, 1967 (Greenway edition). 288 pp.
New York: Dodd, Mead & Co., 1967 (Greenway edition). 288 p.
Leicester, Eng.: Ulverscroft Large Print Edition, 1972. 414 pp.
New York: Garland, 1976 (reprint of 1926 ed.). 305 pp.
See also omnibus editions: *The Agatha Christie Omnibus of Crime; Hercule Poirot: Master Defective; Christie Classics; Masterpieces of Murder; Three Christie Crimes; A Poirot Quintet.*

MURDER ON BOARD (contents: The Mystery of the Blue Train; Death in the Air; What Mrs. McGillicuddy Saw!):

New York: Dodd, Mead & Co., 1974. 601 pp.

MURDER ON THE LINKS:

London: John Lane, 1923. 319 pp.
New York: Dodd, Mead & Co., 1923. 298 pp.
Harmondsworth: Penguin, 1936. 254 pp. (PB)
New York: Dell, 1949. 224 pp. (PB)
London: Corgi Books, 1954. 222 pp. (PB)
London: Bodley Head, 1960. 192 pp.
London: Pan, 1960. 224 pp. (PB)
Leicester, Eng.: Ulverscroft Large Print Edition, 1977. 349 pp.
London: Panther, 1978. 224 pp. (PB)
See also omnibus editions: *An Agatha Christie Omnibus; Two Detective Stories in One Volume.*

MURDER ON THE NILE. A PLAY IN THREE ACTS (dramatization of Death on the Nile):

London: French, 1948. 66 pp.

MURDER ON THE ORIENT EXPRESS:

London: Collins, 1934. 254 pp.
Harmondsworth: Penguin, 1948. 222 pp. (PB)

London: Fontana, 1959. 192 pp. (PB)

Leicester, Eng.: Ulverscroft Large Print Edition, 1965. 253 pp.

London: Collins, 1968 (Greenway edition). 254 pp.

New York: Dodd, Mead & Co., 1968 (Greenway edition). 254 pp.

Leicester, Eng.: Ulverscroft Large Print Edition, 1978. 365 pp.

New York: Pocket Books, 1978. (PB)

—with U.S. title: MURDER IN THE CALAIS COACH:

New York: Dodd, Mead & Co., 1934. 302 pp.

New York: L. E. Spivak. [c. 1934]. 126 pp. (abridged ed.).

New York: Pocket Books, 1940. 246 pp. (PB)

See also omnibus editions: *Hercules Poirot: Master Detective; Three Christie Crimes.*

MURDER PREFERRED (contents: The Patriotic Murders; A Murder Is Announced; Murder in Retrospect):

New York: Dodd, Mead & Co., 1960. 410 pp.

MURDER SHE SAID

see *4.50 from Paddington.*

MURDER WITH MIRRORS

see *They Do It with Mirrors.*

THE MYSTERIOUS AFFAIR AT STYLES:

London & New York: John Lane, 1920. 296 pp.

London: John Lane, 1926. 319 pp.

Harmondsworth: Penguin, 1936. 255 pp. (PB)

New York: Avon Book Co., 1945. 226 pp. (PB)

London: Pan, 1954. 189 pp. (PB)

London: Bodley Head, 1960. 192 pp.

New York: Bantam, 1961. 154 pp. (PB)

London: Longmans, 1965. 181 pp.

New York: Dodd, Mead & Co., 1976 (Commemorative ed.). 239 pp.

New York: G. K. Hall, 1976 (Large Print Books). 351 pp.

London: Panther, 1978. (PB)

See also omnibus editions: *An Agatha Christie Omnibus; Two Detective Stories in One Volume; Curtain and the Mysterious Affair at Styles.*

THE MYSTERIOUS MR. QUIN (short-story collection):

London: Collins, 1930. 287 pp.
New York: Dodd, Mead & Co., 1930. 290 pp.
New York: L. E. Spivak, [c. 1930] 126 pp. (abridged ed.).
New York: Dell, 1950. 256 pp. (PB)
Harmondsworth: Penguin, 1953. 250 pp. (PB)
London: Fontana, 1965. 255 pp. (PB)
London: Pan, 1973. 256 pp. (PB)
Leicester, Eng.: Ulverscroft Large Print Edition, 1977. 456 pp.
See also omnibus editions: *Agatha Christie's Crime Reader; Triple Threat.*

THE MYSTERY OF THE BLUE TRAIN:

London: Collins, 1928. 295 pp.
New York: Dodd, Mead & Co., 1928. 306 pp.
New York: Pocket Books, 1940. 276 pp. (PB)
Harmondsworth: Penguin, 1948. 250 pp. (PB)
London: Fontana, 1958. 248 pp. (PB)
London: Collins, 1972 (Greenway edition). 286 pp.
New York: Dodd, Mead & Co., 1973 (Greenway edition) 286 pp.
Leicester, Eng.: Ulverscroft Large Print Edition, 1976. 423 pp.
See also omnibus editions: *The Agatha Christie Omnibus of Crime; Perilous Journeys of Hercule Poirot; Murder on Board; A Poirot Quintet.*

N OR M?:

London: Collins, 1941. 192 pp.
New York: Dodd, Mead & Co., 1941. 289 pp.
New York: Dell, 1947. 191 pp. (PB)
London: Pan, 1959. 188 pp. (PB)
London: Fontana, 1962. 192 pp. (PB)
London: Collins, 1973 (Greenway edition). 224 pp.
New York: Dodd, Mead & Co., 1974 (Greenway edition). 224 pp.
See also omnibus edition: *Spies among Us.*

NEMESIS:

London: Collins, 1971. 256 pp.
New York: Dodd, Mead & Co., 1971. 271 pp.
New York: Pocket Books, 1973. 229 pp. (PB)
London: Fontana, 1974. 192 pp. (PB)
Leicester, Eng.: Ulverscroft Large Print Edition, 1976. 421 pp.

THE NURSERY RHYME MURDERS (contents: A Pocket Full of Rye; Hickory, Dickory Death; Crooked House):
New York: Dodd, Mead & Co., 1970. 505 pp.

OMNIBUS OF CRIME
see *The Agatha Christie Omnibus of Crime.*

ONE, TWO, BUCKLE MY SHOE:
London: Collins, 1940. 252 pp.
London: Pan, 1956. 192 pp. (PB)
London: Fontana, 1959. 191 pp. (PB)
Leicester, Eng.: Ulverscroft Large Print Edition, 1973. 322 pp.

—with U.S. title: AN OVERDOSE OF DEATH:
New York: Dell, 1953. 192 pp. (PB)

—with U.S. title: THE PATRIOTIC MURDERS:
New York: Dodd, Mead & Co., 1941. 240 pp.
New York: Pocket Books, 1944 (PB)
See also omnibus edition: *Murder Preferred.*

ORDEAL BY INNOCENCE:
London: Collins, 1958. 256 pp.
New York: Dodd, Mead & Co., 1959. 247 pp.
New York: Pocket Books, 1960. 211 pp. (PB)
London: Fontana, 1961. 192 pp. (PB)
Leicester, Eng.: Ulverscroft Large Print Edition, 1964. 256 pp.

AN OVERDOSE OF DEATH
see *One, Two, Buckle My Shoe.*

THE PALE HORSE:
London: Collins, 1961. 256 pp.
New York: Dodd, Mead & Co., 1962. 242 pp.
New York, Pocket Books, 1963. (PB)
London: Fontana, 1964. 191 pp. (PB)
Leicester, Eng.: Ulverscroft Large Print Edition, 1965. 256 pp.

PARKER PYNE INVESTIGATES (short-story collection):
London: Collins, 1934. 248 pp.
Harmondsworth: Penguin, 1953. 190 pp. (PB)

London: Fontana, 1962. 158 pp. (PB)
Leicester, Eng.: Ulverscroft Large Print Edition, 18.

—with U.S. title: MR. PARKER PYNE, DETECTIVE:
New York: Dodd, Mead & Co., 1934. 244 pp.
New York: Dell, 1951. 224 pp. (PB)

PARTNERS IN CRIME (short-story collection):
London: Collins, 1929. 251 pp.
New York: Dodd, Mead & Co., 1929. 277 pp.
New York: L. E. Spivak, [c. 1929]. 126 pp. (abridged ed.).
London: Collins, 1957. 288 pp.
London: Fontana, 1958. 189 pp. (PB)
London: Pan, 1962. 203 pp. (PB)
New York: Dell, 1963. 224 pp. (PB)
See also omnibus editions: *Agatha Christie's Crime Reader; Triple Threat.*

PASSENGER TO FRANKFURT:
London: Collins, 1970. 256 pp.
New York: Dodd, Mead & Co., 1970. 272 pp.
New York: Pocket Books, 1972. (PB)
London: Fontana, 1973. 192 pp. (PB)

THE PATIENT. A PLAY IN ONE ACT:
London: French, 1963. 34 pp.

THE PATRIOTIC MURDERS
see *One, Two, Buckle My Shoe.*

PERIL AT END HOUSE:
London: Collins, 1932. 252 pp.
New York: Dodd, Mead & Co., 1932. 270 pp.
New York: Modern Age Books, 1938. 177 pp.
New York: Pocket Books, 1942. 240 pp. (PB)
Harmondsworth: Penguin, 1948. 204 pp. (PB)
London: Fontana, 1961. 191 pp. (PB)
Leicester, Eng.: Ulverscroft Large Print Edition, 1978.
See also omnibus edition: *Make Mine Murder.*

PERIL AT END HOUSE. A PLAY IN THREE ACTS (dramatization by Arnold Ridley):
London: French, 1945.

PERILOUS JOURNEYS OF HERCULE POIROT (contents: The Mystery of the Blue Train; Death on the Nile; Murder in Mesopotamia):
New York: Dodd, Mead & Co., 1954. Separate pagination.

A POCKET FULL OF RYE:
London: Collins, 1953. 191 pp.
New York: Dodd, Mead & Co., 1954. 211 pp.
New York: Pocket Books, 1955. 186 pp. (PB)
London: Fontana, 1958. 191 pp. (PB)
Leicester, Eng.: Ulverscroft Large Print Edition, 1964. 191 pp.
See also omnibus editions: *The Nursery Rhyme Murders; A Miss Marple Quintet.*

POEMS (vol. 1 [A Masque from Italy], pp. 7–80 of this collection were first published in 1924 under the title The Road of Dreams):
London: Collins, 1973. 124 pp.
New York: Dodd, Mead & Co., 1973. 124 pp.

POIROT INVESTIGATES (short-story collection):
London: John Lane, 1924. 298 pp.
New York: Dodd, Mead & Co., 1925. 282 pp.
London: Pan, 1955. 192 pp. (PB)
New York: Avon, 156 pp. (PB)
New York: Bantam, 1961. 198 pp. (PB)
See also omnibus editions: *An Agatha Christie Omnibus; Agatha Christie's Crime Reader; Triple Threat.*

POIROT KNOWS THE MURDERER (short stories):
London: Polybooks, 1946. 62 pp.

POIROT LENDS A HAND (short stories):
London: Polybooks, 1946. 62 pp.

POIROT LOSES A CLIENT
see *Dumb Witness.*

A POIROT QUINTET (contents: The Murder of Roger Ackroyd; The Mystery of the Blue Train; Dumb Witness; After the Funeral; Death on the Nile):
London: Collins, 1977. 1002 pp.

POIROT'S EARLY CASES (short-story collection; most stories previously published in the U.S. in The Underdog and Other Stories):
London: Collins, 1974. 253 pp.
London: Fontana, 1979. 222 pp. (PB)

—with U.S. title: HERCULE POIROT'S EARLY CASES:
New York: Dodd, Mead & Co., 1974. 250 pp.
New York: G. K. Hall, 1975 (Large Print Books). 491 pp.

POSTERN OF FATE:
London: Collins, 1973. 254 pp.
New York: Dodd, Mead & Co., 1973. 310 pp.
New York: Bantam, 1974. 276 pp. (PB)
New York: G. K. Hall, 1974 (Large Print Books). 471 pp.
London: Fontana, 1976. 221 pp. (PB)

THE RATS. A PLAY IN ONE ACT:
London: French, 1963. 26 pp.

THE REGATTA MYSTERY AND OTHER STORIES:
New York: Dodd, Mead & Co., 1939. 229 pp.
New York: L. E. Spivak, [c. 1939]. 126 pp. (abridged ed.).
New York: Avon, 1946 (PB)
New York: Dell, 1964. 192 pp. (PB)

REMEMBERED DEATH
see Sparkling Cyanide.

THE ROAD OF DREAMS (poems, later republished in Poems):
London: Geoffrey Bles, 1924. 110 pp.

THE ROSE AND THE YEW TREE (Mary Westmacott, pseudonym):
London: Heinemann, 1948. 221 pp.
New York: Rinehart, 1948. 249 pp.

New York: Dell, 1964. 189 pp. (PB)
New York: Arbor House, 1971. 249 pp.
London: Collins, 1973. 190 pp.
London: Fontana, 1974. 192 pp. (PB)
Leicester, Eng: Ulverscroft Large Print Edition, 1978. 358 pp.

RULE OF THREE (plays). Collective title, see: Afternoon at the Sea Side; The
Patient; The Rats.

SAD CYPRESS:
London: Collins, 1940. 252 pp.
New York: Dodd, Mead & Co., 1940. 270 pp.
New York: Dell, 1946. 224 pp. (PB)
London: Fontana, 1959. 191 pp. (PB)
Leicester, Eng.: Ulverscroft Large Print Edition, 1965. 239 pp.
See also omnibus edition: *Make Mine Murder.*

THE SCOOP AND BEHIND THE SCREEN (composite novellas by Christie,
Dorothy L. Sayers, E. C. Bentley, Anthony Berkeley, et al.):
London: Gollancz, 1983, 192 pp.
London: Methuen, 1984, 182 pp.
New York: Harper and Row, 1984, 208 pp.

THE SECRET ADVERSARY:
London & New York: John Lane, 1922. 312 pp.
New York: Dodd, Mead & Co., 1922. 330 pp.
New York: Avon, 1946 (PB)
London, Pan, 1955. 221 pp. (PB)
London: Bodley Head, 1958. 224 pp.
New York: Bantam, 1967. 215 pp. (PB)
London: Panther, 1976. (PB)

THE SECRET OF CHIMNEYS:
London: John Lane, 1925. 306 pp.
New York: Dodd, Mead & Co., 1925. 310 pp.
New York: Dell, 1947. 224 pp. (PB)
London: Pan, 1956. 222 pp. (PB)
London: Bodley Head, 1958. 224 pp.
London: Panther, 1978. 224 pp. (PB)

THE SEVEN DIALS MYSTERY:

> London: Collins, 1929. 276 pp.
> New York: Dodd, Mead & Co., 1929. 310 pp.
> Harmondsworth: Penguin, 1948. 247 pp. (PB)
> London: Fontana, 1954. 189 pp. (PB)
> New York: Avon, 1957 (PB)
> London: Pan, 1962. 207 pp. (PB)
> New York: Bantam, 1964. 184 pp. (PB)
> See also omnibus edition: *The Agatha Christie Omnibus of Crime.*

THE SITTAFORD MYSTERY:

> London: Collins, 1931. 250 pp.
> Harmondsworth: Penguin, 1948. 255 pp. (PB)
> London: Fontana, 1961. 190 pp. (PB)
> Leicester, Eng.: Ulverscroft Large Print Edition, 1973. 387 pp.
> See also omnibus edition: *The Agatha Christie Omnibus of Crime.*

—with United States title: MURDER AT HAZELMOOR:

> New York: Dodd, Mead & Co., 1931. 308 pp.
> New York: Dell, 1950. 224 pp. (PB)

SLEEPING MURDER:

> London: Collins, 1976. 224 pp.
> New York: Dodd, Mead & Co., 1976. 242 pp.
> London: Fontana, 1977. 192 pp. (PB)
> New York: Bantam, 1977. (PB)
> Leicester, Eng.: Ulverscroft Large Print Edition.

SO MANY STEPS TO DEATH

> see *Destination Unknown.*

SPARKLING CYANIDE:

> London: Collins, 1945. 160 pp.
> London: Pan, 1955. 189 pp. (PB)
> London: Fontana, 1960. 189 pp. (PB)
> London: Pan, 1977. 189 pp. (PB)
> Leicester, Eng.: Ulverscroft Large Print Edition.

—with United States title: REMEMBERED DEATH:

> New York: Dodd, Mead & Co., 1945. 209 pp.
> New York: Pocket Books, 1947. (PB)

SPIDER'S WEB. A PLAY IN THREE ACTS:
London: French, 1957. 92 pp.

SPIES AMONG US (contents: They Came to Baghdad; N or M?; Murder in
Mesopotamia):
New York: Dodd, Mead & Co., 1968. 543 pp.

STAR OVER BETHLEHEM AND OTHER STORIES (for children):
London: Collins, 1965. 79 pp.
New York: Dodd, Mead & Co., 1965. 79 pp.

STARRING MISS MARPLE (contents: A Murder Is Announced; The Body
in the Library; Murder with Mirrors):
New York: Dodd, Mead & Co., 1977. Separate pagination.

SURPRISE ENDINGS BY HERCULE POIROT (contents: The ABC Murders;
Murder in Three Acts; Cards on the Table):
New York: Dodd, Mead & Co., 1956. 405 pp.

SURPRISE! SURPRISE! (a collection of mystery stories with unexpected end-
ings, ed. by Raymond T. Bond; all stories previously published):
New York: Dodd, Mead & Co., 1965. 246 pp.
New York: Dell, 1966. 223 pp. (PB)

TAKEN AT THE FLOOD:
London: Collins, 1948. 192 pp.
London: Fontana, 1961. 192 pp. (PB)
London: Pan, 1965. 204 pp. (PB)
Leicester, Eng.: Ulverscroft Large Print Edition, 1971. 386 pp.

—with United States title: THERE IS A TIDE:
New York: Dodd, Mead & Co., 1948. 242 pp.
New York: Pocket Books, 1949 (PB)
New York: Dell, 1955. 224 pp. (PB)

TEN LITTLE INDIANS
see Ten Little Niggers.

TEN LITTLE INDIANS. A MYSTERY PLAY IN THREE ACTS
see Ten Little Niggers. A Play in Three Acts.

TEN LITTLE NIGGERS:

London: Collins, 1939. 252 pp.
London: Pan, 1947. 190 pp. (PB)
Harmondsworth: Penguin, 1958. 201 pp. (PB)
London: Fontana, 1963. 190 pp. (PB)
London: Collins, 1977 (Greenway edition). 252 pp.

—with United States title: AND THEN THERE WERE NONE:

New York: Dodd, Mead & Co., 1940. 264 pp.
New York: Pocket Books, 1944. 173 pp. (PB)
New York: Washington Square Press, 1964 (Teachers ed.). (PB)
See also omnibus editions: *Christie Classics; Masterpieces of Murder.*

—with United States title: TEN LITTLE INDIANS:

New York, Dodd, Mead & Co., 1978 (Greenway edition). 252 pp.

TEN LITTLE NIGGERS. A PLAY IN THREE ACTS.

London: French, 1945. 82 pp.

—with United States title: TEN LITTLE INDIANS. A MYSTERY PLAY IN THREE
ACTS:

New York: French, 1946. 95 pp.
See also: *The Moustrap and Other Plays.*

THERE IS A TIDE

see *Taken at the Flood.*

THEY CAME TO BAGHDAD:

London: Collins, 1951. 256 pp.
New York: Dodd, Mead & Co., 1951. 218 pp.
New York: Pocket Books, 1952. 215 pp. (PB)
London: Fontana, 1957. 192 pp. (PB)
New York: Dell, 1965. 221 pp. (PB)
Leicester, Eng.: Ulverscroft Large Print Edition, 1965. 256 pp.
London: Collins, 1969 (Greenway edition). 287 pp.
New York: Dodd, Mead & Co., 1970 (Greenway edition). 287 pp.
London: Pan, 1974. 221 pp. (PB)
Leicester, Eng.: Ulverscroft Large Print Edition, 1978. 410 pp.
See also omnibus edition: *Spies among Us.*

THEY DO IT WITH MIRRORS:

London: Collins, 1952. 192 pp.

London: Fontana, 1956. 187 pp. (PB)
Leicester, Eng.: Ulverscroft Large Print Edition, 1966. 224 pp.
London: Collins, 1969 (Greenway edition). 223 pp.
New York: Dodd, Mead & Co., 1970 (Greenway edition). 223 pp.
London: Pan, 1971. 187 pp. (PB)
London: Fontana, 1975. 187 pp. (PB)

—with United States title: MURDER WITH MIRRORS:
New York: Dodd, Mead & Co., 1952. 182 pp.
New York: Pocket Books, 1954. 165 pp. (PB)
See also omnibus edition: *Starring Miss Marple.*

THIRD GIRL:
London: Collins, 1966. 256 pp.
New York: Dodd, Mead & Co., 1967. 248 pp.
Leicester, Eng.: Ulverscroft Large Print Edition, 1968. 230 pp.
London: Fontana, 1968. 190 pp. (PB)
New York: Pocket Books, 1968. (PB)

THIRTEEN AT DINNER
see *Lord Edgware Dies.*

THIRTEEN CLUES FOR MISS MARPLE: A COLLECTION OF MYSTERY STORIES (all
previously published):
New York: Dodd, Mead & Co., 1966. 241 pp.
New York: Dell, 1967. 192 pp. (PB)

THIRTEEN FOR LUCK: A SELECTION OF MYSTERY STORIES FOR YOUNG READERS
(all previously published):
New York: Dodd, Mead & Co., 1961. 248 pp.
New York: Dell, 1965. 220 pp. (PB)
London: Collins, 1966. 224 pp.

THE THIRTEEN PROBLEMS (short-story collection):
London: Collins, 1932. 250 pp.
Harmondsworth: Penguin, 1953. 224 pp. (PB)
London: Pan, 1961. 186 pp. (PB)
London: Fontana, 1965. 192 pp. (PB)
Leicester, Eng.: Ulverscroft Large Print Edition, 1968. 207 pp.
London: Collins, 1972 (Greenway edition). 222 pp.
New York: Dodd, Mead & Co., 1973 (Greenway edition). 222 pp.

—with United States title: THE TUESDAY CLUB MURDERS:

New York: Dodd, Mead & Co., 1933. 253 pp.
New York: Avon, 1958 (PB)
New York: Dell, 1963. 192 pp. (PB)

THREE ACT TRAGEDY:

London: Collins, 1935. 252 pp.
London: Fontana, 1957. 192 pp. (PB)
London: Pan, 1964. 203 pp. (PB)
London: Collins, 1972 (Greenway edition). 253 pp.
New York: Dodd, Mead & Co., 1973 (Greenway edition). 253 pp.
Leicester, Eng.: Ulverscroft Large Print Edition, 1975. 351 pp.

—with United States title: MURDER IN THREE ACTS:

New York: Dodd, Mead & Co., 1934. 279 pp.
New York: Avon Book Co., 1945. 230 pp. (PB)
New York: Popular Library, 1961. 175 pp. (PB)
See also omnibus edition: *Surprise Endings by Hercule Poirot.*

THREE BLIND MICE AND OTHER STORIES:

New York: Dodd, Mead & Co., 1950. 250 pp.

—with title: THE MOUSETRAP:

New York: Dell, 1952. 224 pp. (PB)

THREE CHRISTIE CRIMES (contents: The Murder of Roger Ackroyd; Murder in the Calais Coach; Thirteen at Dinner):

New York: Grosset & Dunlap, 1937. Separate pagination.

TOWARDS ZERO:

London: Collins, 1944. 160 pp.
New York: Dodd, Mead & Co., 1944. 242 pp.
New York: Pocket Books, 1947. 210 pp. (PB)
London: Pan, 1948. 195 pp. (PB)
London: Fontana, 1959. 192 pp. (PB)
Leicester, Eng.: Ulverscroft Large Print Edition, 1972. 347 pp.
London: Collins, 1973 (Greenway edition). 224 pp.
New York: Dodd, Mead & Co., 1974 (Greenway edition). 224 pp.
Harmondsworth: Penguin, 1977. 192 pp. (PB)

TOWARDS ZERO. A PLAY IN THREE ACTS (dramatization by Agatha Christie and Gerald Verner):

New York: Dramatists Play Service, 1957. 86 pp.
London: French, 1958. 75 pp.
See also: *The Mousetrap and Other Plays.*

TRIPLE THREAT (contents: Poirot Investigates; The Mysterious Mr. Quin; Partners in Crime):

New York: Dodd, Mead & Co., 1943. Separate pagination.

THE TUESDAY CLUB MURDERS
see *Thirteen Problems.*

TWO DETECTIVE STORIES IN ONE VOLUME (contents: The Mysterious Affair at Styles; The Murder on the Links):

New York: Dodd, Mead & Co., 1940. Separate pagination.

THE UNDERDOG AND OTHER STORIES (all except the title story later published in the United States in *Hercule Poirot's Early Cases*):

New York: Dodd, Mead & Co., 1951. 248 pp.
New York: Pocket Books, 1955. 164 pp. (PB)
New York: Dell, 1965. 192 pp. (PB)

THE UNEXPECTED GUEST. A PLAY IN TWO ACTS:

London: French, 1958. 74 pp.

UNFINISHED PORTRAIT (Mary Westmacott, pseudonym):

New York: Doubleday, 1934. 323 pp.
New York: Dell, 1964. 284 pp. (PB)
New York: Arbor House, 1972. 284 pp.
London: Collins, 1974. 256 pp.

VERDICT. A PLAY IN TWO ACTS:

London: French, 1958. 74 pp.
See also: *The Mousetrap and Other Plays.*

WHAT MRS. MCGILLICUDDY SAW!
see *4.50 from Paddington.*

WHY DIDN'T THEY ASK EVANS?:
    London: Collins, 1934. 252 pp.
    London: Fontana, 1956. 191 pp. (PB)
    London: Collins, 1968 (Greenway edition). 288 pp.
    New York: Dodd, Mead & Co., 1968 (Greenway edition). 288 pp.
    London: Pan, 1968. 188 pp. (PB)
    Leicester, Eng.: Ulverscroft Large Print Edition, 1974. 394 pp.

—with United States title: THE BOOMERANG CLUE:
    New York: Dodd, Mead & Co., 1935. 290 pp.
    New York: Dell, 1944. 224 pp. (PB)

WITNESS FOR THE PROSECUTION. A PLAY IN THREE ACTS:
    London: French, 1954. 74 pp.
    New York: French, 1954. 112 pp.
    London: Fontana, 1958. 127 pp. (PB)
    See also: *The Mousetrap and Other Plays.*

WITNESS FOR THE PROSECUTION AND OTHER STORIES:
    New York: Dodd, Mead & Co., 1948. 272 pp.
    New York: Dell, 1956. 192 pp. (PB)

II
Short-Story Index
(compiled by Louise Barnard)

"ACCIDENT"

PUBLISHED IN:
The Listerdale Mystery (U.K.) 1934
Witness for the Prosecution (U.S.) 1948
13 for Luck (U.S./U.K.) 1961/66

"THE ADVENTURE OF JOHNNIE WAVERLY"

PUBLISHED IN:
Three Blind Mice (U.S.) 1948
The Mousetrap (U.S.) 1965
Surprise! Surprise! (U.S.) 1965
Poirot's Early Cases (U.S.) 1974
Hercule Poirot's Early Cases (U.S.) 1974

"THE ADVENTURE OF THE CHEAP FLAT"

PUBLISHED IN:
Poirot Investigates (U.K./U.S.) 1924
An Agatha Christie Omnibus (U.K.) 1931
Triple Threat (U.S.) 1943
Agatha Christie's Crime Reader (U.S.) 1944

"THE ADVENTURE OF THE CHRISTMAS PUDDING" (slightly different version of
"The Theft of the Royal Ruby")

PUBLISHED IN:

The Adventure of the Christmas Pudding etc. (U.K.) 1960

"THE ADVENTURE OF THE CLAPHAM COOK"
PUBLISHED IN:

The Underdog (U.S.) 1951
Poirot's Early Cases (U.K.) 1974
Hercule Poirot's Early Cases (U.S.) 1974

"THE ADVENTURE OF THE EGYPTIAN TOMB"
PUBLISHED IN:

Poirot Investigates (U.K./U.S.) 1924
An Agatha Christie Omnibus (U.K.) 1931
Triple Threat (U.S.) 1943
Agatha Christie's Crime Reader (U.S.) 1944

"THE ADVENTURE OF THE ITALIAN NOBLEMAN"
PUBLISHED IN:

Poirot Investigates (U.K./U.S.) 1924
An Agatha Christie Omnibus (U.K./U.S.) 1931
Triple Threat (U.S.) 1943

"THE ADVENTURE OF THE SINISTER STRANGER"
PUBLISHED IN:

Partners in Crime (U.K./U.S.) 1929
Triple Threat (U.S.) 1943
Agatha Christie's Crime Reader (U.S.) 1944

"THE ADVENTURE OF 'THE WESTERN STAR'"
PUBLISHED IN:

Poirot Investigates (U.K./U.S.) 1924
An Agatha Christie Omnibus (U.K.) 1931
Triple Threat (U.S.) 1943
Agatha Christie's Crime Reader (U.S.) 1944

"THE AFFAIR AT THE BUNGALOW"
PUBLISHED IN:

Thirteen Problems (U.K.) 1932
The Tuesday Club Murders (U.S.) 1933

"The Affair at the Victory Ball"

PUBLISHED IN:

The Underdog (U.S.) 1951
Poirot's Early Cases (U.K.) 1974
Hercule Poirot's Early Cases (U.S.) 1974

"The Affair of the Pink Pearl"

PUBLISHED IN:

Partners in Crime (U.K./U.S.) 1929
Triple Threat (U.S.) 1943
Agatha Christie's Crime Reader (U.S.) 1944

"The Ambassador's Boots"

PUBLISHED IN:

Partners in Crime (U.K./U.S.) 1929
Triple Threat (U.S.) 1943

"The Apples of the Hesperides"

PUBLISHED IN:

The Labours of Hercules (U.K./U.S.) 1947

"The Arcadian Deer"

PUBLISHED IN:

The Labours of Hercules (U.K./U.S.) 1947
Surprise! Surprise! (U.S.) 1965

"At the Bells and Motley"

PUBLISHED IN:

The Mysterious Mr. Quin (U.K./U.S.) 1930
Triple Threat (U.S.) 1943
Agatha Christie's Crime Reader (U.S.) 1944
Surprise! Surprise! (U.S.) 1965

"The Augean Stables"

PUBLISHED IN:

The Labours of Hercules (U.K./U.S.) 1947

"THE BIRD WITH THE BROKEN WING"
PUBLISHED IN:

> *The Mysterious Mr. Quin* (U.K./U.S.) 1930
> *Triple Threat* (U.S.) 1943
> *13 for Luck* (U.S./U.K.) 1961/66

"BLINDMAN'S BUFF"
PUBLISHED IN:

> *Partners in Crime* (U.K./U.S.) 1929
> *Triple Threat* (U.S.) 1943

"THE BLOOD-STAINED PAVEMENT"
PUBLISHED IN:

> *Thirteen Problems* (U.K.) 1932
> *The Tuesday Club Murders* (U.S.) 1933
> *Thirteen Clues for Miss Marple* (U.S.) 1966

"THE BLUE GERANIUM"
PUBLISHED IN:

> *Thirteen Problems* (U.K.) 1932
> *The Tuesday Club Murders* (U.S.) 1933
> *13 for Luck* (U.S./U.K.) 1961/66
> *Thirteen Clues for Miss Marple* (U.S.) 1966

"THE CALL OF WINGS"
PUBLISHED IN:

> *The Hound of Death* (U.K.) 1933
> *The Golden Ball* (U.S.) 1971

"THE CAPTURE OF CEREBUS"
PUBLISHED IN:

> *The Labours of Hercules* (U.K./U.S.) 1947

"THE CASE OF THE CARETAKER"
PUBLISHED IN:

> *Three Blind Mice* (U.S.) 1948
> *The Mousetrap* (U.S.) 1965

Thirteen Clues for Miss Marple (U.S.) 1966
Miss Marple's Final Cases (U.K.) 1979

"THE CASE OF THE CITY CLERK"
PUBLISHED IN:

Parker Pyne Investigates (U.K.) 1934
Mr. Parker Pyne, Detective (U.S.) 1934

"THE CASE OF THE DISCONTENTED HUSBAND"
PUBLISHED IN:

Parker Pyne Investigates (U.K.) 1934
Mr. Parker Pyne, Detective (U.S.) 1934

"THE CASE OF THE DISCONTENTED SOLDIER"
PUBLISHED IN:

Parker Pyne Investigates (U.K.) 1934
Mr. Parker Pyne, Detective (U.S.) 1934

"THE CASE OF THE DISTRESED LADY"
PUBLISHED IN:

Parker Pyne Investigates (U.K.) 1934
Mr. Parker Pyne, Detective (U.S.) 1934
Surprise! Surprise! (U.S.) 1965

"THE CASE OF THE MIDDLE AGED WIFE"
PUBLISHED IN:

Parker Pyne Investigates (U.K.) 1934
Mr. Parker Pyne, Detective (U.S.) 1934

"THE CASE OF THE MISSING LADY"
PUBLISHED IN:

Partners in Crime (U.K./U.S.) 1929
Triple Threat (U.S.) 1943
Agatha Christie's Crime Reader (U.S.) 1944

"The Case of the Missing Will"
PUBLISHED IN:

> *Poirot Investigates* (U.K./U.S.) 1924
> *An Agatha Christie Omnibus* (U.K.) 1931
> *Triple Threat* (U.S.) 1943

"The Case of the Perfect Maid"
PUBLISHED IN:

> *Three Blind Mice* (U.S.) 1948
> *The Mousetrap* (U.S.) 1965
> *Surprise! Surprise!* (U.S.) 1965
> *Thirteen Clues for Miss Marple* (U.S.) 1966
> *Miss Marple's Final Cases* (U.K.) 1979

"The Case of the Retired Jeweller"

(alternative title for "The Tape-Measure Murder")

"The Case of the Rich Woman"
PUBLISHED IN:

> *Parker Pyne Investigates* (U.K.) 1934
> *Mr. Parker Pyne, Detective* (U.S.) 1934

"The Chess Problem"

(see *The Big Four*, chapter 11; sometimes published separately)

"The Chocolate Box"
PUBLISHED IN:

> *Poirot Investigates* (U.S. ed. only) 1925
> *Triple Threat* (U.S.) 1943
> *Poirot's Early Cases* (U.K.) 1974
> *Hercule Poirot's Early Cases* (U.S.) 1974

"A Christmas Tragedy"
PUBLISHED IN:

> *Thirteen Problems* (U.K.) 1932
> *The Tuesday Club Murders* (U.S.) 1933

"THE CLERGYMAN'S DAUGHTER"

PUBLISHED IN:

> *Partners in Crime* (U.K./U.S.) 1929
> *Triple Threat* (U.S.) 1943

"THE COMING OF MR. QUIN"

PUBLISHED IN:

> *The Mysterious Mr. Quin* (U.K./U.S.) 1930
> *Triple Threat* (U.S.) 1943
> *Agatha Christie's Crime Reader* (U.S.) 1944

"THE COMPANION"

PUBLISHED IN:

> *Thirteen Problems* (U.K.) 1932
> *The Tuesday Club Murders* (U.S.) 1933
> *Thirteen Clues for Miss Marple* (U.S.) 1966

"THE CORNISH MYSTERY"

PUBLISHED IN:

> *The Underdog* (U.S.) 1951
> *Surprise! Surprise!* (U.S.) 1965
> *Poirot's Early Cases* (U.K.) 1974
> *Hercule Poirot's Early Cases* (U.S.) 1974

"THE CRACKLER"

PUBLISHED IN:

> *Partners in Crime* (U.K./U.S.) 1929
> *Triple Threat* (U.S.) 1943

"THE CRETAN BULL"

PUBLISHED IN:

> *The Labours of Hercules* (U.K./U.S.) 1947

"THE DEAD HARLEQUIN"

PUBLISHED IN:

> *The Mysterious Mr. Quin* (U.K./U.S.) 1930
> *Triple Threat* (U.S.) 1943

"Dead Man's Mirror" (expanded version of "The Second Gong")
PUBLISHED IN:

Murder in the Mews (U.K.) 1937
Dead Man's Mirror etc. (U.S.) 1937

"Death by Drowning"
PUBLISHED IN:

Thirteen Problems (U.K.) 1932
The Tuesday Club Murders (U.S.) 1933

"Death on the Nile"
PUBLISHED IN:

Parker Pyne Investigates (U.K.) 1934
Mr. Parker Pyne, Detective (U.S.) 1934

"The Disappearance of Mr. Davenheim"
PUBLISHED IN:

Poirot Investigates (U.K./U.S.) 1924
An Agatha Christie Omnibus (U.K.) 1931
Triple Threat (U.S.) 1943

"The Disappearance of Mrs. Leigh Gordon"
(alternative title for "The Case of the Missing Lady")

"The Double Clue"
PUBLISHED IN:

Double Sin (U.S.) 1961
Poirot's Early Cases (U.K.) 1974
Hercule Poirot's Early Cases (U.S.) 1974

"Double Sin"
PUBLISHED IN:

Double Sin etc. (U.S.) 1961
Surprise! Surprise! (U.S.) 1965
Poirot's Early Cases (U.K.) 1974
Hercule Poirot's Early Cases (U.S.) 1974

"THE DREAM"

PUBLISHED IN:

The Regatta Mystery (U.S.) 1939
The Adventure of the Christmas Pudding (U.K.) 1960

"THE DRESSMAKER'S DOLL"

PUBLISHED IN:

Double Sin (U.S.) 1961
Miss Marple's Final Cases (U.K.) 1979

"THE ERYMANTHIAN BOAR"

PUBLISHED IN:

The Labours of Hercules (U.K./U.S.) 1947

"THE FACE OF HELEN"

PUBLISHED IN:

The Mysterious Mr. Quin (U.K./U.S.) 1930
Triple Threat (U.S.) 1943
13 for Luck (U.K./U.S.) 1961/66

"FINESSING THE KING"

PUBLISHED IN:

Partners in Crime (U.K./U.S.) 1929
Triple Threat (U.S.) 1943
Agatha Christie's Crime Reader (U.S.) 1944

"THE FLOCK OF GERYON"

PUBLISHED IN:

The Labours of Hercules (U.K./U.S.) 1947

"FOUR-AND-TWENTY BLACKBIRDS"

PUBLISHED IN:

Three Blind Mice (U.S.) 1948
The Adventure of the Christmas Pudding (U.K.) 1960
The Mousetrap (U.S.) 1965

"THE FOUR SUSPECTS"

PUBLISHED IN:

> *Thirteen Problems* (U.K.) 1932
> *The Tuesday Club Murders* (U.S.) 1933
> *13 for Luck* (U.S./U.K.) 1961/66
> *Thirteen Clues for Miss Marple* (U.S.) 1966

"THE FOURTH MAN"

PUBLISHED IN:

> *The Hound of Death* (U.K.) 1933
> *Witness for the Prosecution* (U.S.) 1948

"A FRUITFUL SUNDAY"

PUBLISHED IN:

> *The Listerdale Mystery* (U.K.) 1934
> *The Golden Ball* (U.S.) 1971

"THE GATE OF BAGHDAD"

PUBLISHED IN:

> *Parker Pyne Investigates* (U.K.) 1934
> *Mr. Parker Pyne, Detective* (U.S.) 1934

"THE GENTLEMAN DRESSED IN NEWSPAPER"

PUBLISHED IN:

> *Partners in Crime* (U.K./U.S.) 1929
> *Triple Threat* (U.S.) 1943
> *Agatha Christie's Crime Reader* (U.S.) 1944

"THE GIPSY"

PUBLISHED IN:

> *The Hound of Death* (U.K.) 1933
> *The Golden Ball* (U.S.) 1971

"THE GIRDLE OF HYPPOLITA"

PUBLISHED IN:

> *The Labours of Hercules* (U.K./U.S.) 1947
> *13 for Luck* (U.S./U.K.) 1961/66

"The Girl in the Train"

PUBLISHED IN:

The Listerdale Mystery (U.K.) 1934
The Golden Ball (U.S.) 1971

"The Golden Ball"

PUBLISHED IN:

The Listerdale Mystery (U.K.) 1934
The Golden Ball etc. (U.S.) 1971

"Greenshaw's Folly"

PUBLISHED IN:

The Adventure of the Christmas Pudding (U.K.) 1960
Double Sin (U.S.) 1961
Surprise! Surprise! (U.S.) 1965
Thirteen Clues for Miss Marple (U.S.) 1966

"The Harlequin Tea Set"

PUBLISHED IN:

Hardinge, George, ed.: Winter's Crimes 3 (London: Macmillan, 1971)
Ellery Queen's Murdercade (London: Gollancz, 1975)

"Harlequin's Lane"

PUBLISHED IN:

The Mysterious Mr. Quin (U.K./U.S.) 1930
Triple Threat (U.S.) 1943

"Have You Got Everything You Want?"

PUBLISHED IN:

Parker Pyne Investigates (U.K.) 1934
Mr. Parker Pyne, Detective (U.S.) 1934

"The Herb of Death"

PUBLISHED IN:

Thirteen Problems (U.K.) 1932
The Tuesday Club Murders (U.S.) 1933
Thirteen Clues for Miss Marple (U.S.) 1966

"THE HORSES OF DIOMEDES"
PUBLISHED IN:

> *The Labours of Hercules* (U.K./U.S.) 1947

"THE HOUND OF DEATH"
PUBLISHED IN:

> *The Hound of Death etc.* (U.K.) 1933
> *The Golden Ball* (U.S.) 1971

"THE HOUSE AT SHIRAZ"
PUBLISHED IN:

> *Parker Pyne Investigates* (U.K.) 1934
> *Mr. Parker Pyne, Detective* (U.S.) 1934

"THE HOUSE OF LURKING DEATH"
PUBLISHED IN:

> *Partners in Crime* (U.K./U.S.) 1929
> *Triple Threat* (U.S.) 1943

"HOW DOES YOUR GARDEN GROW?"
PUBLISHED IN:

> *The Regatta Mystery* (U.S.) 1939
> *Poirot's Early Cases* (U.K.) 1974
> *Hercule Poirot's Early Cases* (U.S.) 1974

"THE IDOL HOUSE OF ASTARTE"
PUBLISHED IN:

> *Thirteen Problems* (U.K.) 1932
> *The Tuesday Club Murders* (U.S.) 1933

"IN A GLASS DARKLY"
PUBLISHED IN:

> *The Regatta Mystery* (U.S.) 1939
> *Miss Marple's Final Cases* (U.K.) 1979

"The Incredible Theft" (expanded version of "The Submarine Plans")
PUBLISHED IN:

Murder in the Mews (U.K.) 1937

"Ingots of Gold"
PUBLISHED IN:

Thirteen Problems (U.K.) 1932
The Tuesday Club Murders (U.S.) 1933

"Jane in Search of a Job"
PUBLISHED IN:

The Listerdale Mystery (U.K.) 1934
The Golden Ball (U.S.) 1971

"The Jewel Robbery at the Grand Metropolitan"
PUBLISHED IN:

Poirot Investigates (U.K./U.S.) 1924
An Agatha Christie Omnibus (U.K.) 1931
Triple Threat (U.S.) 1943

"The Kidnapped Prime Minister"
PUBLISHED IN:

Poirot Investigates (U.K./U.S.) 1924
An Agatha Christie Omnibus (U.K.) 1931
Triple Threat (U.S.) 1943

"The Kidnapping of Johnnie Waverly"
(alternative title for "The Adventure of Johnnie Waverly")

"The King of Clubs"
PUBLISHED IN:

The Underdog (U.S.) 1951
Poirot's Early Cases (U.K.) 1974
Hercule Poirots's Early Cases (U.S.) 1974

"THE LAMP"

PUBLISHED IN:

The Hound of Death (U.K.) 1933
The Golden Ball (U.S.) 1971

"THE LAST SEANCE"

PUBLISHED IN:

The Hound of Death (U.K.) 1933
Double Sin (U.S.) 1961

"THE LEMESURIER INHERITANCE"

PUBLISHED IN:

The Underdog (U.S.) 1951
Poirot's Early Cases (U.K.) 1974
Hercule Poirot's Early Cases (U.S.) 1974

"THE LERNEAN HYDRA"

PUBLISHED IN:

The Labours of Hercules (U.K./U.S.) 1947

"THE LISTERDALE MYSTERY"

PUBLISHED IN:

The Listerdale Mystery etc. (U.K.) 1934
The Golden Ball (U.S.) 1971

"THE LOST MINE"

PUBLISHED IN:

Poirot Investigates (U.S. ed. only) 1925
Triple Threat (U.S.) 1943
Poirot's Early Cases (U.K.) 1974
Hercule Poirot's Early Cases (U.S.) 1974

"THE LOVE DETECTIVES"

PUBLISHED IN:

Three Blind Mice (U.S.) 1948
The Mousetrap (U.S.) 1965

"Magnolia Blossom"

PUBLISHED IN:

>The Golden Ball (U.S.) 1971

"The Man from the Sea"

PUBLISHED IN:

>The Mysterious Mr. Quin (U.K./U.S.) 1930
>Triple Threat (U.S.) 1943

"The Man in the Mist"

PUBLISHED IN:

>Partners in Crime (U.K./U.S.) 1929
>Triple Threat (U.S.) 1943

"The Man Who Was No. 16"

PUBLISHED IN:

>Partners in Crime (U.K./U.S.) 1929
>Triple Threat (U.S.) 1943

"The Manhood of Edward Robinson"

PUBLISHED IN:

>The Listerdale Mystery (U.K.) 1934
>The Golden Ball (U.S.) 1971

"The Market Basing Mystery"

PUBLISHED IN:

>The Underdog (U.S.) 1951
>13 for Luck (U.S./U.K.) 1961/66
>Poirot's Early Cases (U.K.) 1974
>Hercule Poirot's Early Cases (U.S.) 1974

"The Million Dollar Bond Robbery"

PUBLISHED IN:

>Poirot Investigates (U.K./U.S.) 1924
>An Agatha Christie Omnibus (U.K.) 1931
>Triple Threat (U.S.) 1943
>Agatha Christie's Crime Reader (U.S.) 1944

"Miss Marple Tells a Story"
PUBLISHED IN:

> *The Regatta Mystery* (U.S.) 1939
> *Miss Marple's Final Cases* (U.K.) 1979

"Mr. Eastwood's Adventure"
PUBLISHED IN:

> *The Listerdale Mystery* (U.K.) 1934

"Motive vs. Opportunity"
PUBLISHED IN:

> *Thirteen Problems* (U.K.) 1932
> *The Tuesday Club Murders* (U.S.) 1933
> *Thirteen Clues for Miss Marple* (U.S.) 1966

"Murder in the Mews"
PUBLISHED IN:

> *Murder in the Mews etc.* (U.K.) 1937
> *Dead Man's Mirror* (U.S.) 1937

"The Mystery of the Baghdad Chest" (see also expanded version with title "The Mystery of the Spanish Chest")
PUBLISHED IN:

> *The Regatta Mystery* (U.S.) 1939
> *Poirot Knows the Murderer* (U.K.) 1946

"The Mystery of the Blue Jar"
PUBLISHED IN:

> *The Hound of Death* (U.K.) 1933
> *Witness for the Prosecution* (U.S.) 1948

"The Mystery of the Crime in Cabin 66"
PUBLISHED IN:

> *Poirot Knows the Murderer* (U.K.) 1946

"The Mystery of Hunter's Lodge"
PUBLISHED IN:

Poirot Investigates (U.K./U.S.) 1924
An Agatha Christie Omnibus (U.K.) 1931
Triple Threat (U.S.) 1943
Agatha Christie's Crime Reader (U.S.) 1944

"The Mystery of the Spanish Chest" (slightly expanded version of "The Mystery of the Baghdad Chest")
PUBLISHED IN:

The Adventure of the Christmas Pudding (U.K.) 1960

"The Mystery of the Spanish Shawl" (alternative title for "Mr. Eastwood's Adventure")
PUBLISHED IN:

Witness for the Prosecution (U.S.) 1948
Surprise! Surprise! (U.S.) 1965

"The Nemean Lion"
PUBLISHED IN:

The Labours of Hercules (U.K./U.S.) 1947
13 for Luck (U.S./U.K.) 1961/66

"Next to a Dog"
PUBLISHED IN:

The Golden Ball (U.S.) 1971

"The Oracle at Delphi"
PUBLISHED IN:

Parker Pyne Investigates (U.K.) 1934
Mr. Parker Pyne, Detective (U.S.) 1934

"The Pearl of Price"
PUBLISHED IN:

Parker Pyne Investigates (U.K.) 1934
Mr. Parker Pyne, Detective (U.S.) 1934

"THE PERFECT MAID"

(alternative title for "The Case of the Perfect Maid")

"PHILOMEL COTTAGE"

PUBLISHED IN:

> *The Listerdale Mystery* (U.K.) 1934
> *Witness for the Prosecution* (U.S.) 1948
> *Christie Classics* (U.S.) 1957

"THE PLYMOUTH EXPRESS"

PUBLISHED IN:

> *The Underdog* (U.S.) 1951
> *Surprise! Surprise!* (U.S.) 1965
> *Poirot's Early Cases* (U.K.) 1974
> *Hercule Poirot's Early Cases* (U.S.) 1974

"PROBLEM AT POLLENSA BAY"

PUBLISHED IN:

> *The Regatta Mystery* (U.S.) 1939
> *Poirot Lends a Hand* (U.K.) 1946
> *13 for Luck* (U.S./U.K.) 1961/66

"PROBLEM AT SEA"

PUBLISHED IN:

> *The Regatta Mystery* (U.S.) 1939
> *Poirot's Early Cases* (U.K.) 1974
> *Hercule Poirot's Early Cases* (U.S.) 1974

"THE RAJAH'S EMERALD"

PUBLISHED IN:

> *The Listerdale Mystery* (U.K.) 1934
> *The Golden Ball* (U.S.) 1971

"THE RED HOUSE"

PUBLISHED IN:

> *Partners in Crime* (U.K./U.S.) 1929
> *Triple Threat* (U.S.) 1943

"THE RED SIGNAL"

PUBLISHED IN:

> *The Hound of Death* (U.K.) 1933
> *Witness for the Prosecution* (U.S.) 1948

"THE REGATTA MYSTERY"

PUBLISHED IN:

> *The Regatta Mystery etc.* (U.S.) 1939
> *Poirot on Holiday* (U.K.) 1943
> *Poirot Lends a Hand* (U.K.) 1946
> *13 for Luck* (U.S./U.K.) 1961/66

"SANCTUARY"

PUBLISHED IN:

> *Double Sin* (U.S.) 1961
> *Thirteen Clues for Miss Marple* (U.S.) 1966
> *Miss Marple's Final Cases* (U.K.) 1979

"THE SECOND GONG" (see also expanded version with title "Dead Man's Mirror")

PUBLISHED IN:

> *Witness for the Prosecution* (U.S.) 1948

"THE SHADOW ON THE GLASS"

PUBLISHED IN:

> *The Mysterious Mr. Quin* (U.K./U.S.) 1930
> *Triple Threat* (U.S.) 1943
> *Agatha Christie's Crime Reader* (U.S.) 1944

"THE SIGN IN THE SKY"

PUBLISHED IN:

> *The Mysterious Mr. Quin* (U.K./U.S.) 1930
> *Triple Threat* (U.S.) 1943

"SING A SONG OF SIXPENCE"

PUBLISHED IN:

> *The Listerdale Mystery* (U.K.) 1934

"SIREN BUSINESS"

(alternative title for "Problem at Pollensa Bay")

"SOS"

PUBLISHED IN:

The Hound of Death (U.K.) 1933
Witness for the Prosecution (U.S.) 1948

"THE SOUL OF THE CROUPIER"

PUBLISHED IN:

The Mysterious Mr. Quin (U.K./U.S.) 1930
Triple Threat (U.S.) 1943
Agatha Christie's Crime Reader (U.S.) 1944

"THE STRANGE CASE OF SIR ANDREW CARMICHAEL"

PUBLISHED IN:

The Hound of Death (U.K./U.S.) 1933
The Golden Ball (U.S.) 1971

"STRANGE JEST"

PUBLISHED IN:

Three Blind Mice (U.S.) 1948
The Mousetrap (U.S.) 1965
Thirteen Clues for Miss Marple (U.S.) 1966
Miss Marple's Final Cases (U.K.) 1979

"THE STYMPHALEAN BIRDS"

PUBLISHED IN:

The Labours of Hercules (U.K./U.S.) 1947

"THE SUBMARINE PLANS" (see also expanded version with title "The
Incredible Theft")

PUBLISHED IN:

The Underdog (U.S.) 1951
Poirot's Early Cases (U.K.) 1974
Hercule Poirot's Early Cases (U.S.) 1974

"THE SUNNINGDALE MYSTERY"

PUBLISHED IN:

> *Partners in Crime* (U.K./U.S.) 1929
> *Triple Threat* (U.S.) 1943

"SWAN SONG"

PUBLISHED IN:

> *The Listerdale Mystery* (U.K.) 1934
> *The Golden Ball* (U.S.) 1971

"THE TAPE-MEASURE MURDER"

PUBLISHED IN:

> *Three Blind Mice* (U.S.) 1948
> *13 for Luck* (U.S./U.K.) 1961/66
> *The Mousetrap* (U.S.) 1965
> *Thirteen Clues for Miss Marple* (U.S.) 1966
> *Miss Marple's Final Cases* (U.K.) 1979

"THEFT OF THE ROYAL RUBY" (slightly different version of "The Adventure of the Christmas Pudding")

PUBLISHED IN:

> *Double Sin* (U.S.) 1961

"THE THIRD FLOOR FLAT"

PUBLISHED IN:

> *Three Blind Mice* (U.S.) 1948
> *The Mousetrap* (U.S.) 1965
> *Surprise! Surprise!* (U.S.) 1965
> *Poirot's Early Cases* (U.K.) 1974
> *Hercule Poirot's Early Cases* (U.S.) 1974

"THREE BLIND MICE"

PUBLISHED IN:

> *Three Blind Mice etc.* (U.S.) 1948
> *Christie Classics* (U.S.) 1957
> *The Mousetrap* (U.S.) 1965

"THE THUMB MARK OF SAINT PETER"

PUBLISHED IN:

Thirteen Problems (U.K.) 1932
The Tuesday Club Murders (U.S.) 1933
Thirteen Clues for Miss Marple (U.S.) 1966

"THE TRAGEDY OF MARSDON MANOR"

PUBLISHED IN:

Poirot Investigates (U.K./U.S.) 1924
An Agatha Christie Omnibus (U.K.) 1931
Triple Threat (U.S.) 1943
Agatha Christie's Crime Reader (U.S.) 1944

"TRIANGLE AT RHODES"

PUBLISHED IN:

Murder in the Mews (U.K.) 1937
Dead Man's Mirror (U.S.) 1937

"THE TUESDAY NIGHT CLUB"

PUBLISHED IN:

Thirteen Problems (U.K.) 1932
The Tuesday Club Murders (U.S.) 1933

"THE UNBREAKABLE ALIBI"

PUBLISHED IN:

Partners in Crime (U.K./U.S.) 1929
Triple Threat (U.S.) 1943
13 for Luck (U.S./U.K.) 1961/66

"THE UNDERDOG"

PUBLISHED IN:

The Underdog etc. (U.S.) 1951
The Adventure of the Christmas Pudding (U.K.) 1960

"THE VEILED LADY"

PUBLISHED IN:

Poirot Investigates (U.S. ed. only) 1925
Triple Threat (U.S.) 1943

Poirot Lends a Hand (U.K.) 1946
13 for Luck (U.S./U.K.) 1961/66
Poirot's Early Cases (U.K.) 1974
Hercule Poirot's Early Cases (U.S.) 1974

"A VILLAGE MURDER"

(alternative title for "The Tape-Measure Murder")

"THE VOICE IN THE DARK"

PUBLISHED IN:

The Mysterious Mr. Quin (U.K./U.S.) 1930
Triple Threat (U.S.) 1943

"WASPS' NEST"

PUBLISHED IN:

Double Sin (U.S.) 1961
Poirot's Early Cases (U.K.) 1974
Hercule Poirot's Early Cases (U.S.) 1974

"THE WATER BUS"

(alternative title for "Star Over Bethlehem")

"WHERE THERE'S A WILL" (alternative title for "Wireless")

PUBLISHED IN:

Witness for the Prosecution (U.S.) 1948
Surprise! Surprise! (U.S.) 1965

"WIRELESS"

PUBLISHED IN:

The Hound of Death (U.K.) 1933

"THE WITNESS FOR THE PROSECUTION"

PUBLISHED IN:

The Hound of Death (U.K.) 1933
Witness for the Prosecution etc. (U.S.) 1948
Christie Classics (U.S.) 1957
Surprise! Surprise! (U.S.) 1965
Masterpieces of Murder (U.S.) 1977

"THE WORLDS END"

PUBLISHED IN:

> *The Mysterious Mr. Quin* (U.K./U.S.) 1930
> *Triple Threat* (U.S.) 1943
> *Agatha Christie's Crime Reader* (U.S.) 1944

"YELLOW IRIS"

PUBLISHED IN:

> *The Regatta Mystery* (U.S.) 1939

III
Secondary Sources

A. Books About Agatha Christie

There are, to my knowledge, seven books dealing with Agatha Christie and her novels. They are:

Behre, Frank. *Studies in Agatha Christie's Writings* (Göteborg, 1967).
Feinman, J. *The Mysterious World of Agatha Christie* (New York, 1975).
Keating, H. R. F., ed. *Agatha Christie. First Lady of Crime* (London, 1977).
Murdoch, Derrick. *The Agatha Christie Mystery* (New York, 1976).
Ramsey, G. C. *Agatha Christie. Mistress of Mystery* (London, 1968; New York, 1967).
Robyns, Gwen. *The Mystery of Agatha Christie* (New York, 1978).
Wynne, Nancy Blue. *An Agatha Christie Chronology* (New York, 1976).

Of these, Behre is a (misleadingly titled) study in linguistics of interest only to grammarians; Keating is an excellent and varied anthology of essays, with particularly interesting contributions from Julian Symons, Emma Lathen and Michael Gilbert; Murdoch is an intelligent and good-humored account of Christie's life (now superseded by *An Autobiography*) and her place in the history of detective fiction; Ramsey is a tribute which looked old-fashioned at the time it came out, and now seems positively prehistoric; Robyns is a short, unauthorized biography, so execrably written as to make one appreciate, by comparison, Christie's own penny-plain style; Wynne is useful (but *not* infallible) bibliographically. I have not been able to look at the Feinman volume.

NOTE

Since the first, hardcover edition of this book appeared, a number of books about Agatha Christie have been published. The most valuable are:

Morgan, Janet. *Agatha Christie* (London, 1984, New York, 1985). The authorized biography: warm, perceptive, enlightening, though not always reliable on the books.

Bargainnier, Earl F. *The Gentle Art of Murder* (Bowling Green, 1980). Full, fair assessment of her craft, if slightly plodding.

Osborne, Charles. *The Life and Crimes of Agatha Christie* (London, 1982, New York, 1983). Pleasant, sometimes nit-picking, sometimes inaccurate run-through of the works. Better written and less embarrassing than his other writings might lead one to expect.

Sanders, Dennis, and Lovallo, Len. *The Agatha Christie Companion* (New York, 1984, London 1986). Ill-organized. Interesting information on trains, boats and other background stuff.

B. Articles, Essays and Parts of Books about Agatha Christie and the "Golden Age" of British Detective Fiction

This is not the place for an extensive bibliography of books and articles about crime fiction. For that, the reader can go to the Cawelti or Palmer titles mentioned below, or to Barzun's *Catalogue of Crime*. What I have included here are studies (most of them fairly recent) which I have found interesting and stimulating in writing this book, and which I think the committed reader will find profitable. An extensive list of secondary material on Christie will be found in "Agatha Christie: A First Checklist of Secondary Sources," by William White, in the *Bulletin of Bibliography* 36, no. 1 (January–March, 1979).

(Anonymous). "Commentary," in *Times Literary Supplement,* September 18, 1970.

Auden, W. H. "The Guilty Vicarage," in *The Dyer's Hand* (London, 1963).

Barzun, J. and Taylor, W.H. *A Catalogue of Crime* (New York, 1971).

Barzun, J. "Detection in Extremis," in *Crime in Good Company,* ed. Michael Gilbert (London, 1959).

Barzun, J. "The Novel Turns Tale," in *Mosaic* IV, no. 3 (University of Manitoba Press).

Calder, R. "Agatha and I," in *New Statesman,* January 30, 1976.

Green, M. *Translatlantic Patterns* (New York, 1977).

Cawelti, J. G. *Adventure, Mystery and Romance* (Chicago, 1976).

Grella, G. "Murder and Manners: the Formal Detective Story," in *Novel* 4 (1970).

Gwilt, P. R. and J. R. "Dame Agatha's Poisonous Pharmacopoeia," in *The Pharmaceutical Journal*, December 23 and 30, 1978.

Keating, H. R. F., ed. *Crime Writers* (London, BBC, 1978).

Kissane, J. and J. M. "Sherlock Holmes and the Ritual of Reason," in *Nineteenth Century Fiction 17* (March 1963).

Kitchin, C. H. B. "Five Writers in One: The Versatility of Agatha Christie," in *Times Literary Supplement*, February 25, 1955.

La Cour, T., Mogensen, H. and Larsen, E. *Dansk og Udenlansk Kriminallitteratur* (Copenhagen, 1975).

Palmer, J. *Thrillers* (London, 1978).

Ritchie, J. "Agatha Christie's England, 1918–1939," in *Australian National University's Historical Journal 9* (December 1972).

Symons, J. *Bloody Murder* (London, 1972; revised ed. Harmondsworth, 1974).

Watson, C. *Snobbery with Violence* (London, 1971).

Wilson, E. "Why Do People Read Detective Stories?" and "Who Cares Who Killed Roger Ackroyd?" in *Classics and Commercials* (New York, 1950).

IV
Annotated List

What follows is a brief commentary on all the full-length works with detective interest that Agatha Christie published. For the reader's convenience I have included alternative American titles, the date of first publication in Great Britain, the nature of the volume (novel, play, short story, etc.) and the name of the principal detective if he is a recurring figure in Christie's works (though in the short-story collections I have named the detective only if he or she appears in all or most of the stories). I have omitted plays adapted from her novels.

The ABC Murders
[1936: Novel: Poirot]
   A classic, still fresh story, beautifully worked out. It differs from the usual pattern in that we *seem* to be involved in a chase: the series of murders *appears* to be the work of a maniac. In fact the solution reasserts the classic pattern of a closed circle of suspects, with a logical, well-motivated murder plan. The English detective story cannot embrace the irrational, it seems. A total success—but thank God she didn't try taking it through to Z. Analyzed at length in Ramsey, *Agatha Christie: Mistress of Mystery.*

The Adventure of the Christmas Pudding
[1960: Short Stories]
   A late collection, with several of the "long-short" stories which suit Christie well. Less rigorous than her best, however, and the last story, "Greenshaw's Folly," has a notable example of Miss Marple's habit of drawing solutions from a hat, with hardly a trace of why or wherefore.

After the Funeral
(U.S.: *Funerals Are Fatal*)
[1953: Novel: Poirot]

A subject of perennial appeal—unhappy families: lots of scattered siblings, lots of Victorian money (made from corn plasters). Be sure you are investigating the right murder, and watch for mirrors (always interesting in Christie). Contains Christie's last major butler: the 'fifties and 'sixties were not good times for butlers.

Appointment with Death
[1938: Novel: Poirot]

Notable example of classic-era Christie, with excellent Near East setting, and repulsive matriarch as victim. The family tensions around her are conveyed more involvingly than usual. The detection, with its emphasis on who-was-where-and-when, is a little too like Ngaio Marsh of the period, and there is some vagueness in the motivation, but this is as taut and atmospheric as any she wrote, and should film well. Note the lady MP: how Christie did dislike professional women!

At Bertram's Hotel
[1965: Novel: Miss Marple]

The plot rather creaky, as in most of the late ones, but the hotel atmosphere is very well conveyed and used (see chapter V, above). Elvira Blake is one of the best observed of the many young people in late Christie. Note the reflections in chapter 5 in the novel on the changed look of elderly people, showing that the sharp eye had not dimmed, even if the narrative grasp was becoming shaky.

The Big Four
[1927: Novel: Poirot]

This thriller was cobbled together at the lowest point in Christie's life, with the help of her brother-in-law. Charity is therefore the order of the day, and is needed, for this is pretty dreadful, and (whatever one may think of him as a creation) demeaning to Poirot.

The Body in the Library
[1942: Novel: Miss Marple]

Bravura performance on a classic situation. St. Mary Mead regulars figure in the case, pleasantly diversified by fashionable seaside hotel guests and the film crowd. If you think what happens to the body after death is unlikely, try the more "realistic" P. D. James' *An Unsuitable Job for a*

Woman. Christie's remarks in her foreword about her inability to create characters from people she knows is surely a mite disingenuous?

By the Pricking of My Thumbs
[1968: Novel: Tommy and Tuppence]
Begins rather well, with a vicious old aunt of Tommy's in a genteel old people's home, but declines rapidly into a welter of half-realized plots and a plethora of those conversations, all too familiar in late Christie, which meander on through irrelevancies, repetitions and inconsequentialities to end nowhere (as if she had sat at the feet of Samuel Beckett). Makes one appreciate the economy of the dialogue—all point, or at least possible point—in early Christie.

Cards on the Table
[1936: Novel: Poirot]
On the very top rung. Special opportunities for bridge enthusiasts, but others can play. Mr. Shaitana, a man of peculiar tastes, invites four murderers and four crime experts to dinner, and the latter notably fail to prevent one of the former perpetrating the expected. Superb tight construction and excellent clueing. Historians of Poirot's career will have to address themselves to the puzzling question of which came first, this case or the ABC Murders (see chapter II here, and *ABC*, chapter 3). Battle, Race and Mrs. Oliver tag along. Will be read as long as hard-faced ladies gather for cards.

A Caribbean Mystery
[1964: Novel: Miss Marple]
In the tradition of all those package-tour mysteries written by indigent crime writers who have to capitalize on their meager holidays. Nothing much of interest, but useful for illustrating the "fluffification" of Miss Marple. The reflections (p. 1) on Anglo-Indian colonels show how little she felt she had to change her stereotypes to bring them up to date. Re-uses a ploy from *Appointment with Death.*

Cat among the Pigeons
[1959: Novel: Poirot]
Girls' school background surprisingly well done, with humor and some liberality of outlook. Some elements are reminiscent of Tey's *Miss Pym Disposes.* Marred by the international dimension and the spy element, which do not jell with the traditional detective side. Fairly typical example of her looser, more relaxed later style.

The Clocks
[1963: Novel: Poirot]

Lively, well-narrated, highly unlikely late specimen—you have to accept two spies and three murderers living in one small-town crescent. The business of the clocks, fantastic and intriguing in itself, fizzles out miserably at the end. Contains (chapter 14) Poirot's considered reflections on other fictional detectives, and the various styles and national schools of crime writing.

Crooked House
[1949: Novel]

"Pure pleasure" was how the author described the writing of this, which was long planned, and remained one of her favorites. As the title implies, this is a family murder—and a very odd family indeed. The solution, one of the classic ones, was anticipated (but much less effectively) in Allingham's 'prentice work *The White Cottage Mystery.*

Curtain
[1975: Novel: Poirot]

Written in the 'forties, designed for publication after Christie's death, but in fact issued just before it. Based on an idea toyed with in *Peril at End House* (chapter 9)—a clever and interesting one, but needing greater subtlety in the handling than Christie's style or characterization will allow (the characters here are in any case quite exceptionally pallid). In fact, for a long-cherished idea, and as an exit for Poirot, this is oddly perfunctory in execution.

Dead Man's Folly
[1956: Novel: Poirot]

Highly traditional recipe, but not done with the same conviction as in the 'thirties. Nobody much is what they seem, and old sins cast long shadows. Mrs. Oliver looms large here, as she was frequently to do from now on, both in Poirot books and in others.

Death Comes as the End
[1945: Novel]

Hercule Poirot's Christmas, transported to Egypt, ca. 2000 B.C. Done with tact, yet the result is somehow skeletal—one realizes how much the average Christie depends on trappings: clothes, furniture, the paraphernalia of bourgeois living. The culprit in this one is revealed less by detection than by a process of elimination.

Death in the Clouds
(U.S.: *Death in the Air*)
[1935: Novel: Poirot]

Exceptionally lively specimen, with wider than usual class- and type-range of suspects. Scrupulously fair, with each clue presented openly and discussed. Note Clancy the crime writer, and the superiority of French police to British (no signs of insularity here). Notice too the list of likes and dislikes (cf. similar list in *Autobiography*) with, under latter heading, "Negroes."

Death on the Nile
[1937: Novel: Poirot]

One of the top ten, in spite of an overcomplex solution. The familiar marital triangle, set on a Nile steamer. Comparatively little local color, but some good grotesques among the passengers—of which the film took advantage. Spies and agitators are beginning to invade the pure Christie detective story at this period, as the slide toward war begins.

Destination Unknown
(U.S.: *So Many Steps to Death*)
[1954: Novel]

Slightly above-average thriller, with excellent beginning (heroine, whose husband has left her for another woman, and whose small daughter has died, contemplates suicide in strange hotel). Thereafter topples over into hokum, with a notably unexciting climax. Mainly concerns disappearing scientists—it was written in the wake of the Fuchs/Pontecorvo affairs. Mentions the un-American Activities Committee, without obvious disapproval.

Double Sin
[U.S.: 1961: Short Stories]

American short-story collection, published in various British volumes, including the posthumous *Miss Marple's Final Cases*. "The Theft of the Royal Ruby" is basically identical with "The Adventure of the Christmas Pudding." "Sanctuary" includes some characters from *A Murder Is Announced*.

Dumb Witness
(U.S.: *Poirot Loses a Client*)
[1937: Novel: Poirot]

Not quite vintage for the period: none of the relations of the dead woman is particularly interesting, and the major clue is very obvious. The doggy stuff is rather embarrassing, though done with affection and knowledge. At the end the dog is given to Hastings—or possibly vice versa. Exit Hastings, until *Curtain*.

Elephants Can Remember
[1972: Novel: Poirot]

Another murder-in-the-past case, with nobody able to remember anything clearly, including, alas, the author. At one time we are told that General Ravenscroft and his wife (the dead pair) were respectively sixty and thirty-five; later we are told he had fallen in love with his wife's twin sister "as a young man." The murder/suicide is once said to have taken place ten to twelve years before, elsewhere fifteen, or twenty. Acres of meandering conversations, hundreds of speeches beginning with "Well, . . ." That sort of thing may happen in life, but one doesn't want to read it.

Endless Night
[1967: Novel]

The best of the late Christies, the plot a combination of patterns used in *Ackroyd* and *Nile* (note similarities in treatment of heiress/heroine's American lawyers in *Nile* and here, suggesting she had been rereading). The murder occurs very late, and thus the central section seems desultory, even novelettish (poor little rich girl, gypsy's curse, etc.). But all is justified by the conclusion. A splendid late flowering.

Evil under the Sun
[1941: Novel: Poirot]

The classic Christie marital triangle plot (see chapter VI, above) set in West Country seaside resort, with particular play on the alikeness of sunbathing bodies, and dead ones. Possibly overingenious and slightly undercharacterized, but colorful and ripe (one gathers) for filming.

Five Little Pigs
(U.S.: *Murder in Retrospect*)
[1943: Novel: Poirot]

The murder-in-the-past plot on its first and best appearance—accept no later substitutes. Presentation more intricate than usual, characterization more subtle. See also chapter VII, above.

4.50 from Paddington
(U.S.: *What Mrs. McGillicuddy Saw!*)
[1957: Novel: Miss Marple]

Another locomotive one—murder seen as two trains pass each other in the same direction. Later settles down into a good old family murder. Contains one of Christie's few sympathetic independent women. Miss Marple apparently solves the crime by divine guidance, for there is very little in the way of clues or logical deduction.

The Golden Ball
[U.S.: 1971: Short Stories]

An American collection, consisting mainly of stories published in Britain in *The Listerdale Mystery* and *Hound of Death* collections. The exceptions are "Magnolia Blossom" and "Next to a Dog," which are not detective stories, and are unlikely to be published in Britain.

Hallowe'en Party
[1969: Novel: Poirot]

Bobbing for apples turns serious when ghastly child is extinguished in the bucket. The plot of this late one is not too bad, but the telling is very poor: it is littered with loose ends, unrealized characters, and maintains only a marginal hold on the reader's interest. Much of it reads as if spoken into a tape-recorder and never read through afterward.

Hercule Poirot's Christmas
(U.S.: *Murder for Christmas*)
[1938: Novel: Poirot]

Welcome interruption to the festive season as mischievous old patriarch, tyrant and sinner gets his deserts. Magnificently clued. See chapter VII, above.

Hickory, Dickory Dock
(U.S.: *Hickory, Dickory Death*)
[1955: Novel: Poirot]

A significant falling-off in standards in this mid-'fifties story. A highly perfunctory going-through-the-paces: the rhyme has no meaning within the story; the plot (drugs smuggled in imported haversacks) is unlikely in the extreme; and the attempt to widen the range of character types (Africans, Indians, students of Freud etc.) is far from successful. Evelyn Waugh's diary records that it "began well" but deteriorated "a third of the way through into twaddle"—a judgment which, unusual for him, erred on the side of charity.

The Hollow
[1946: Novel: Poirot]

Notable specimen, with more complex characterization than usual, and occasionally rising to wit (especially on the subject of cooking). Illustrates vividly one dilemma of the detective writer: if you establish characters of some psychological complexity, how do you prevent the routine detection stuff coming as an anticlimax? Christie records that her daughter protested against her decision to dramatize the book, and the instinct was probably right: most of the interest here, unusually, is internal, and difficult to present via Christie's rather old-fashioned stage techniques.

Definitely among the top ten, in spite of the falling-off in the second half.

The Hound of Death
[1933: Short Stories]

Mostly semisupernatural stories. In this setting, "Witness for the Prosecution" stands out as the jewel it is: surely this is the cleverest short story she wrote. Of the others, the best is perhaps "The Call of Wings," but that, depressingly, was one of the very first things she wrote (pre-World War I). In this mode she got no better.

The Labours of Hercules
[1947: Short Stories: Poirot]

Probably the best single short-story collection, because more varied in its problems and lighter in its touch than usual. Lots of tricks from her novels, and other people's, used very skillfully. But the mention of a goblet made by Cellini for Alexander VI (before the age of three?) is a good example of Christie slapdashness, almost amounting to philistinism or contempt for her audience.

The Listerdale Mystery
[1934: Short Stories]

Most of the stories in this collection are "jolly," rather than detection. The final story is a dreadfully obvious one based on *Tosca*. The two stories with detective interest are the often reprinted "Philomel Cottage" (good, but rather novelettish in style), and the clever "Accident."

Lord Edgware Dies
(U.S.: *Thirteen at Dinner*)
[1933: Novel: Poirot]

Deals with a social/artistic milieu rather off Christie's usual beat: aristocrats, actresses, socialities, rich Jews. The anti-Semitism is more muted than in the early thrillers, but still leaves a nasty taste (this is the last book in which it obtrudes). Otherwise clever and unusual, with the Hastings/

Poirot relationship done less crudely than usual. The central idea came from watching Ruth Draper.

The Man in the Brown Suit
[1924: Novel: Colonel Race]

Written during and about a trip to Southern Africa, this opens attractively with the heroine and her archeologist father (Agatha's interest in the subject was obviously pre-Max), and has some pleasant interludes with the diary of the baddie. But it degenerates into the usual stuff of her thrillers, and the plot would probably not bear close examination, if anyone were to take the trouble. First appearance of Colonel Race, who pops up not very interestingly in several later books, for example *Death on the Nile*.

The Mirror Crack'd from Side to Side
(U.S.: *The Mirror Crack'd*)
[1962: Novel: Miss Marple]

The last of the true English village mysteries in Christie's output, and one of the best of her later books. Film milieu superimposed on the familiar St. Mary Mead background. Like most Marples this is not rich in clueing, but the changes in village life and class structure since the war are detailed in a knowledgeable and fairly sympathetic way. *Ave Atque Vale,* Mayhem Parva!

Miss Marple's Final Cases
[1979: Short stories: Miss Marple]

Posthumous collection, containing several good and goodish Marple cases previously only available in the States. "Sanctuary" contains characters from *A Murder Is Announced*. Also two supernatural stories, which Christie did not have the stylistic resources to bring off successfully.

Mrs. McGinty's Dead
[1952: Novel: Poirot]

This village murder begins among the rural proletariat (cf. "Death by Drowning" in *Thirteen Problems* and the excellent London working-class women in *The Hollow*), but after a time it moves toward the better-spoken classes. Poirot suffers in a vividly awful country guesthouse in order to get in with the community and rescue a rather unsatisfactory young man from the gallows. Highly ingenious—at this point she is still able to vary the tricks she plays, not repeat them.

The Moving Finger
[1943: Novel: Miss Marple]

Poison pen in Mayhem Parva, inevitably leading to murder. A good and varied cast list, some humor, and stronger than usual romantic interest of an ugly-duckling-into-swan type. One of the few times Christie gives short measure, and none the worse for that.

American readers should note that almost all U.S. editions consist of a shorter and revised version of the novel, presumably prepared for magazine publication. It is very inferior to the British version.

The Murder at the Vicarage
[1930: Novel: Miss Marple]

Our first glimpse of St. Mary Mead, a hotbed of burglary, impersonation, adultery and ultimately murder. What is it precisely that people find so cosy about such stories? The solution boggles the mind somewhat, but there are too many incidental pleasures to complain, and the strong dose of vinegar in this first sketch of Miss Marple is more to modern taste than the touch of syrup in later presentations.

Murder in Mesopotamia
[1936: Novel: Poirot]

Archeological dig provides unusual setting, expertly and entertainingly presented. Wife-victim surely based on Katherine Woolley (see descriptions in *Autobiography*), and very well done. Narrated by nurse, a temporary Hastings-substitute—soon she found she could do without such a figure altogether. Marred by an ending which goes beyond the improbable to the inconceivable.

Murder in the Mews
(U.S.: *Dead Man's Mirror*)
[1937: Short Stories: Poirot]

Four very good long short stories. No duds, but perhaps the most interesting is "Triangle at Rhodes," with its "double-triangle" plot, very familiar from other Christies. The American version of the book lacks "The Incredible Theft," which does not seem ever to have been published in the States, though a shorter version of it, "The Submarine Plans," was.

A Murder Is Announced
[1950: Novel: Miss Marple]

Superb reworking of standard Christie setting and procedures, marred only by an excess of homicide at the end. The book is distantly related to the story "The Companion," in *Thirteen Problems*. See chapter VII, above.

Murder Is Easy
(U.S.: *Easy to Kill*)
[1939: Novel: Superintendent Battle]

Archetypal Mayhem Parva story, with all the best ingredients: Cranford-style village with "about six women to every man"; doctors, lawyers, retired colonels and antique dealers; suspicions of black magic; and, as optional extra ingredient, a memorably awful press lord. And of course a generous allowance of sharp old spinsters. Shorter than most on detection, perhaps because the detection is, until the end, basically amateur. One of the classics.

The Murder of Roger Ackroyd
[1926: Novel: Poirot]

Apart—and it is an enormous "apart"—from the sensational solution, this is a fairly conventional Christie. The tone is light, at times almost "comedy of manners"; the setting is English village, with the emphasis on the big house; the characterization is standard, with the first and best of her strong-minded spinsters, noses aquiver for scandal. A classic, but there are some better Christies.

Murder on the Links
[1923: Novel: Poirot]

Supercomplicated early whodunit, set in the northerly fringes of France so beloved of the English bankrupt. Poirot pits his wits against a sneering sophisticate of a French policeman, while Hastings lets his wander after an auburn-haired female acrobat. Entertaining for most of its length, but the solution is one of those "once revealed, instantly forgotten" ones, where ingenuity has triumphed over common sense. See also chapter III, above.

Murder on the Orient Express
(U.S.: *Murder in the Calais Coach*)
[1934: Novel: Poirot]

The best of the railway stories. The Orient Express, snowed up in Yugoslavia, provides the ideal "closed" setup for a classic-style exercise in detection, as well as an excuse for an international cast-list. Contains my favorite line in all Christie: "Poor creature, she's a Swede." Impeccably clued, with a clever use of the Cyrilic alphabet (cf. "The Double Clue"). The solution roused the ire of Raymond Chandler, but won't bother anyone who doesn't insist his detective fiction mirror real-life crime.

The Mysterious Affair at Styles
[1920: Novel: Poirot]

Christie's debut novel, from which she made £25 and John Lane made goodness knows how much. The Big House in wartime, with privations, war work and rumors of spies. Her hand was overliberal with clues and red herrings, but it was a highly cunning hand, even at this stage. See also chapter III, above.

The Mysterious Mr. Quin
[1930: Short Stories: Mr. Harley Quin]

An odd collection, with the whimsical-supernatural element strong, though not unpleasing. There are some notably dreadful stories ("Bird with a Broken Wing," "Voice in the Dark"), but the unusual number of erudite or cultural references bears witness to Christie's own opinion of these stories—they were aimed more "up-market" than usual. Quin did not become a fixture in her work, but appears in another short story, "The Love Detectives," so far unpublished in Britain, and also the late "Harlequin Tea Set."

The Mystery of the Blue Train
[1928: Novel: Poirot]

Christie's least favorite story, which she struggled with just before and after the disappearance. The international setting makes for a good varied read, but there is a plethora of sixth-form schoolgirl French and some deleterious influences from the thrillers. There are several fruitier candidates for the title of "worst Christie."

N or M?
[1941: Novel: Tommy and Tuppence]

The Beresfords contribute their intolerable high spirits to the war effort. Less racist than the earlier thrillers (in fact, some apology is made indirectly) but no more convincing.

Nemesis
[1971: Novel: Miss Marple]

Miss Marple is sent on a tour of stately gardens by Mr. Rafiel (of *A Caribbean Mystery*). The garden paths we are led up are neither enticing nor profitable. All the usual strictures about late Christie apply.

One, Two, Buckle My Shoe
(U.S.: *The Patriotic Murders*)
[1940: Novel: Poirot]

It is usually said that Christie drags herself into the modern world in the 'fifties, but the books in the late 'thirties show her dipping a not-too-confident toe into the ideological conflicts of the prewar years. Here we have political "idealists," fascist movements and conservative financiers who maintain world stability. But behind it all is a fairly conventional murder mystery, beguilingly and cunningly sustained. See also chapter V, above.

Ordeal by Innocence
[1958: Novel]

One of the best of 'fifties Christies, and one of her own favorites (though she named different titles at different times). The *Five Little Pigs* pattern of murder-in-the-past, the convicted murderer having died in prison, innocent. Short on detection, but fairly dense in social observation. Understanding in treatment of adopted children, but not altogether tactful on the color question: "Tina's always the dark horse. . . . Perhaps it's the half of her that isn't white."

The Pale Horse
[1961: Novel: Mrs. Oliver]

Goodish late example—loosely plotted, but with an intriguing, fantastical central idea. Plot concerns a Murder-Inc.-type organization, with a strong overlay of black magic. Also makes use of "The Box," a piece of pseudo-scientific hocus-pocus fashionable in the West Country in the 'fifties (one of the things that drove Waugh to the verge of lunacy, as narrated in *Pinfold*). Some old friends from vintage Christie turn up: Mrs. Dane Calthrop (from *Moving Finger*) and Rhoda Dawes and Major Despard (from *Cards*, the only time an earlier suspect is reused).

Parker Pyne Investigates
(U.S.: *Mr. Parker Pyne, Detective*)
[1934: Short Stories: Parker Pyne]

A mediocre collection. Parker Pyne begins as a consultant Miss Lonely-hearts, ends up as a conventional detective. Pyne also reappears in "Problem at Pollensa Bay," a story not as yet published in Britain. Brief first appearance of Mrs. Oliver.

Partners in Crime
[1929: Short Stories: Tommy and Tuppence]

Tommy and Tuppence in a series of short stories which parody detective writers and their methods. Many of these are long forgotten, but the parodies are not sharp enough for this to matter very much. "The House of Lurking Death" anticipates the solution of Sayers's *Strong Poison.*

Passenger to Frankfurt
[1970: Novel]

The last of the thrillers, and one that slides from the unlikely to the inconceivable and finally lands up in incomprehensible muddle. Prizes should be offered to readers who can explain the ending. Concerns the youth uproar of the 'sixties, drugs, a new Aryan superman and so on, subjects of which Christie's grasp was, to say the least, uncertain (she seems to have the oddest idea of what the term "Third World" means, for example). Collins insisted she subtitle the book "An Extravaganza." One can think of other descriptions.

Peril at End House
[1932: Novel: Poirot]

A cunning use of simple tricks used over and over in Christie's career (be careful, for example, about names—diminutives and ambiguous male-female Christian names are always possibilities as reader-deceivers). Some creaking in the machinery, and rather a lot of melodrama and improbabilities, prevent this from being one of the very best of the classic specimens.

A Pocket Full of Rye
[1953: Novel: Miss Marple]

Super-stockbrokerbelt setting, and quite exceptionally nasty family of suspects. (Christie usually prefers to keep most of her characters at least *potentially* sympathetic as well as potential murderers, but here they are only the latter). Something of a rerun of *Hercule Poirot's Christmas* (loathsome father, goody-goody son, ne'er-do-well son, gold-digger wife, etc.), but without its tight construction and ingenuity. And the rhyme is an irrelevancy. Still, a good, sour read.

Poirot Investigates
[1924: Short Stories: Poirot]

Early stories, written very much under the shadow of Holmes and Watson. The tricks are rather repetitive and the problems lack variety. The American edition includes three stories not in the British one, but these were later included in *Poirot's Early Cases.*

Poirot's Early Cases
(U.S. *Hercule Poirot's Early Cases*)
[1974: Short Stories: Poirot]

A late collection of early stories (mostly from the 'twenties), which had been published in the States but not in Britain. This may suggest discarded chips from the workshop, but in fact the standard here is distinctly higher than in the stories in *Poirot Investigates*, which were the ones Christie did publish in Britain at the time. Note that "The Submarine Plans" was later expanded into "The Incredible Theft," and the situation in "The Plymouth Express" was also used in *The Mystery of the Blue Train*.

Postern of Fate
[1973: Novel: Tommy and Tuppence]

The last book Christie wrote. Best (and easily) forgotten.

The Regatta Mystery
[U.S.: 1939: Short Stories]

A miscellaneous American collection, including many stories not published in Britain until the posthumous collection of 1979. Worth acquiring, since "Yellow Iris" will not be published in Britain (it anticipates the solution of *Sparkling Cyanide*).

Rule of Three
[1963: Plays]

Christie's farewell to the theater: three one-acters, of which "The Patient" is effective, with some good, dry dialogue, and "Rats" is an excellent piece of screw-turning (it uses some ideas from "The Mystery of the Spanish Chest"). "Afternoon at the Seaside" would need *very* sharp professional performances to bring it off: death for amateurs.

Sad Cypress
[1940: Novel: Poirot]

A variation on the usual triangle theme, and the only time Christie uses the lovely-woman-in-the-dock-accused-of-murder ploy. Elegiac, more emotionally involving than is usual in Christie, but the ingenuity and superb clueing put it among the very best of the classic titles. Her knowledge of poison is well to the fore, but the amateur will also benefit from a knowledge of horticulture and a skill in close reading.

The Secret Adversary
[1922: Novel: Tommy and Tuppence]

The first and best (no extravagant compliment, this) of the Tommy and

Tuppence stories. It tells how the dauntless pair foils a plot to foment labor unrest and red revolution in Britain, masterminded by the man *behind* the Bolshevists. Good reactionary fun, if you're in that mood. See also chapter II, above.

The Secret of Chimneys
[1925: Novel: Superintendent Battle]

If you can take all the racialist remarks, which are very much of their time, this is a first-class romp, all the better for not being of the "plot to take over the world" variety. It concerns the throne and crown jewels of Herzoslovakia, and combines such Hope-ful elements with bright young things and some effective caricatures. By far the least awful of the early thrillers. See also chapter II, above.

The Seven Dials Mystery
[1929: Novel: Superintendent Battle]

Shares characters and setting with *Chimneys*, but without the same verve and cheek.

The Sittaford Mystery
(U.S.: *Murder at Hazelmoor*)
[1931: Novel]

Mayhem Parva, sharpened by Dartmoor setting and snow. Many of the usual elements are here, but also escaped convict (out of *Baskervilles*), séances, newspaper competitions and amateur investigator—young woman torn (as in *Blue Train*) between handsome weakling and hardworking, upright, born-to-success type. Highly entertaining, with adroit clueing.

Sleeping Murder
[1976: Novel: Miss Marple]

Slightly somniferous mystery, written in the 'forties but published after Christie's death. Concerns a house where murder has been committed, bought (by the merest coincidence) by someone who as a child saw the body. Sounds like Ross Macdonald, and certainly doesn't read like vintage Christie. But why would an astute businesswoman hold back one of her better performances for posthumous publication?

Sparkling Cyanide
(U.S.: *Remembered Death*)
[1945: Novel: Colonel Race]

Murder in the past, previously accepted as suicide. Upper-class tart gets her come-uppance in smart London restaurant, and husband later suffers the same fate. Compulsively told, the strategies of deception smart as a new pin, and generally well up to 'forties standard. But the solution takes more swallowing than cyanided champagne.

Spider's Web
[1957: Play]

A comedy thriller, rather short on both comedy and thrills. Written for Margaret Lockwood, but probably now best left for Little Puddleton rep in the silly season.

Taken at the Flood
(U.S.: *There Is a Tide*)
[1948: Novel: Poirot]

Elderly man married to glamorous nitwit of dubious social background is a common plot-element in Christie. Here she is widowed (in an air-raid—this is one of the few Christies anchored to an actual time), and burdened by financially insatiable relatives, both of blood and in-law. But who exactly is dead, and who isn't? And who is what they seem, and who isn't? Compulsive reworking of Tennysonian and Christiean themes, and pretty high up in the range of classic titles.

Ten Little Niggers
(U.S.: *And Then There Were None*)
[1939: Novel]

Unusually suspenseful and menacing detective-story-cum-thriller. The closed setting with the succession of deaths is here taken to its logical conclusion, and the dangers of ludicrousness and sheer reader-disbelief are skillfully avoided. Probably the best-known Christie, and justifiably among the most popular.

They Came to Baghdad
[1951: Novel]

Fairly preposterous example of thriller-type Christie, but livelier than some. Engaging heroine and unusually good minor characters—archeologists, hotelkeeper etc. The plot concerns attempts to prevent The Big Three (Britain was one of them then) from coming together and making peace. Though the villains are not left-wing, they sound like her left-wing idealists of the 'thirties (wanting, as usual, to create a "New Heaven and Earth"—highly dangerous!).

They Do It with Mirrors
(U.S.: *Murder with Mirrors*)
[1952: Novel: Miss Marple]

Unusual (and not entirely convincing) setting of delinquents' home, full of untrustworthy adolescents and untrustworthy do-gooders. Christie obviously not entirely at home, perhaps because she believes (in Miss Marple's words) that "young people with a good heredity, and brought up wisely in a good home . . . they are really . . . the sort of people a country *needs*." Otherwise highly traditional, with house-plans, Marsh-y inquisitions, and second and third murders done most perfunctorily. Definite signs of decline.

Third Girl
[1966: Novel: Poirot]

One of Christie's more embarrassing attempts to haul herself abreast of the swinging 'sixties. Mrs. Oliver plays a large part, detection a small one. Analyzed at length in Cawelti's *Adventure, Mystery and Romance*.

The Thirteen Problems
(U.S.: *The Tuesday Club Murders*)
[1932: Short Stories: Miss Marple]

Early Marple, in which she solves cases described by other amateur and professional murder buffs gathered in an ad hoc club. Some engaging stories, but the sedentary format (cf. Orczy's "Old Man in the Corner" stories) becomes monotonous over the book length. Contains one of Christie's few excursions into the working class, "Death by Drowning."

Three Act Tragedy
(U.S.: *Murder in Three Acts*)
[1935: Novel: Poirot]

The strategy of deception here is one that by this date ought to have been familiar to Christie readers. This is perhaps not one of the best examples of the trick, because few of the characters other than the murderer are well individualized. The social mix here is more artistic and sophisticated than is usual in Christie.

American readers should note that in U.S. editions the motive for the murders has been changed, presumably by Christie's American publishers, to the book's detriment.

Three Blind Mice
[U.S.: 1950: Short Stories]

A good collection, published only in America, containing the long short story which is the origin of *The Mousetrap,* unpublished in Britain in her lifetime, presumably lest it shortened the mind-boggling run. Also contains several good Marple stories unpublished in Britain until the posthumous *Miss Marple's Final Cases.*

Towards Zero
[1944: Novel: Superintendent Battle]
  Superb: intricately plotted and unusual. The murder comes late, and the real climax of the murderer's plot only at the end. The ingenuity excuses a degree of far-fetchedness. Highly effective story of the child and the bow-and-arrow (part II, chapter 6) and good characterization of the playboy-sportsman central character—very much of that era when one was expected to behave like a gentleman at Wimbledon.

The Underdog
[U.S. 1951: Short Stories]
  An American collection, the title story of which appeared in Britain in *The Adventure of the Christmas Pudding,* all the rest in *Poirot's Early Cases.*

The Unexpected Guest
[1958: Play]
  Unexpectedly good, with some effective, dry dialogue at the beginning and more nervous tension—genuine emotional tension—than in most of her plays. To characterize the dead man she uses incidents from late in the career of her erratic brother Monty (see *Autobiography,* [Fontana], p. 336), though there seems no general resemblance. As the play concerns in part a prominent West Country Liberal involved in a murder case, it is not surprising it was revived for a successful tour in 1978.

Verdict
[1958: Play]
  Bloomsbury setting for a play centering on a conflict of consciences, with little detective interest. Unsuccessful with the public, but Christie's favorite of her own plays.

Why Didn't They Ask Evans?
  (U.S.: *The Boomerang Clue*)
[1934: Novel]
  Lively, with occasional glimpses of a *Vile Bodies* world, though one short on Waugh's anarchic humor and long on snobbery ("Nobody looks at a chauffeur the way they look at a person"). Weakened by lack of proper

detective: the investigating pair are bumbling amateurs, with more than a touch of Tommy and Tuppence.

Witness for the Prosecution
[U.S.: 1948: Short Stories]

An American collection, containing stories available in Britain in *The Hound of Death* and *The Listerdale Mystery*. The only story unpublished in Britain, "The Second Gong," is a shorter version of "Dead Man's Mirror," one of the long short stories in *Murder in the Mews*.

V
The Christie Films

1928   *Die Abenteuer G.m.b.H.*
      Source: *The Secret Adversary*
      Director: Fred Sauer
      Stars: Eve Gray; Carlo Aldini; Michael Rasumny.

1928   *The Passing of Mr Quinn* [sic]
      Source: "The Coming of Mr. Quin" in *The Mysterious Mr. Quin*
      Director: Leslie Hiscott
      Screenplay: Leslie Hiscott
      Stars: Stewart Rome; Ursula Jeans; Trilby Clark.

1931   *Alibi*
      Source: the play *Alibi*, a dramatization by Michael Morton of *The Murder of Roger Ackroyd*
      Director: Leslie Hiscott
      Stars: Austin Trevor (Poirot); Franklin Dyall (Ackroyd); Elizabeth Allan.

1931   *Black Coffee*
       Source: the play of the same name
       Director: Leslie Hiscott
       Stars: Austin Trevor; Richard Cooper (Hastings); Adrienne Allen;
           Melville Cooper (Japp); Dino Galvani.

1934   *Lord Edgware Dies*
       Source: the novel of the same name
       Director: Henry Edwards
       Stars: Austin Trevor; Jane Carr; Melville Cooper; John Turnbull
           (Japp).

1937   *Love from a Stranger*
       Source: the play of the same name by Frank Vosper, a dramatization
           of "Philomel Cottage" in *The Listerdale Mystery*
       Director: Rowland V. Lee
       Screenplay: Frances Marion
       Stars: Ann Harding; Basil Rathbone.

1945   *And Then There Were None* (in U.K. *Ten Little Niggers*)
       Source: the play *Ten Little Niggers,* from the novel of the same name
       Director: René Clair
       Stars: Barry Fitzgerald; Walter Houston; C. Aubrey Smith; Judith
           Anderson; Roland Young; Mischa Auer; June Duprez; Louis
           Hayward.

1947   *Love from a Stranger* (in U.K. *A Stranger Passes*)
       Source: see above under 1937 version
       Director: Richard Whorf
       Screenplay: Philip MacDonald
       Stars: Sylvia Sidney; John Hodiak.

1957   *Witness for the Prosecution*
       Source: the play of the same name, from the story of the same
           name in *The Hound of Death*

Director: Billy Wilder
Screenplay: Billy Wilder and Harry Kurnitz
Stars: Tyrone Power; Marlene Dietrich: Charles Laughton; Elsa Lanchester.

1960 *The Spider's Web*
Source: the play *Spider's Web*
Director: Godfrey Grayson
Stars: Glynis Johns; Cicely Courtneidge; Jack Hulbert; David Nixon; John Justin; Peter Butterworth.

1962 *Murder She Said*
Source: *4.50 from Paddington*
Director: George Pollock
Screenplay: David Pursall and Jack Seddon
Stars: Margaret Rutherford (Miss Marple); Muriel Pavlow; James Robertson Justice; Ronald Howard; Stringer Davis.

1963 *Murder at the Gallop*
Source: *After the Funeral*
Director: George Pollock
Screenplay: James Cavenaugh
Stars: Margaret Rutherford; Flora Robson; Robert Morley; Stringer Davis.

1964 *Murder Most Foul*
Source: *Mrs. McGinty's Dead*
Director: George Pollock
Screenplay: David Pursall and Jack Seddon
Stars: Margaret Rutherford; Ron Moody; Charles Tingwell, Megs Jenkins; Stringer Davis.

1964 *Murder Ahoy!*
Source: the only Christiean element is the character of Miss Marple, as interpreted by Margaret Rutherford

Director: George Pollock
Screenplay: David Pursall and Jack Seddon
Stars: Margaret Rutherford; Lionel Jeffries; Charles Tingwell; String-
er Davis.

1965 *Ten Little Indians*
Source: the play *Ten Little Niggers,* from the novel of the same name
Director: George Pollock
Stars: Dennis Price; Leo Genn; Shirley Eaton; Stanley Holloway;
Wilfred Hyde White

1966 *The Alphabet Murders*
Source: *The ABC Murders*
Director: Frank Tashlin
Screenplay: David Pursall and Jack Seddon
Stars: Tony Randall (Poirot); Robert Morley (Hastings); Anita Ekberg;
Maurice Denham.

1971 *Endless Night*
Source: the novel of the same name
Director: Sidney Gilliat
Screenplay: Sidney Gilliat
Stars: Hayley Mills; Hywel Bennett; Per Oscarsson; Britt Ekland;
George Sanders.

1974 *Murder on the Orient Express*
Source: the novel of the same name
Director: Sidney Lumet
Screenplay: Paul Dehn
Stars: Albert Finney (Poirot); Lauren Bacall; Martin Balsam; Ingrid
Bergman; Sean Connery; John Gielgud; Wendy Hiller; Anthony
Perkins; Vanessa Redgrave; Rachel Roberts; Richard Widmark.

1975 *Ten Little Indians* (in U.K. *And Then There Were None*)
Source: the play *Ten Little Niggers,* from the novel of the same name

Director: Peter Collinson
Stars: Oliver Reed; Richard Attenborough; Herbert Lom; Elke Sommer;
    Charles Aznavour.

1978 *Death on the Nile*
Source: the novel of the same name
Director: Don Guillermin
Screenplay: Anthony Shaffer
Stars: Peter Ustinov (Poirot); Bette Davis; Angela Lansbury; Maggie
    Smith; David Niven; Jon Finch; Mia Farrow.

1980 *The Mirror Crack'd*
Source: *The Mirror Crack'd from Side to Side*
Director: Guy Hamilton
Screenplay: Anthony Shaffer
Stars: Elizabeth Taylor; Kim Novak; Rock Hudson; Angela Lansbury;
    Tony Curtis; Edward Fox.

1982 *Evil Under the Sun*
Source: the novel of the same name
Director: Guy Hamilton
Screenplay: Anthony Shaffer
Stars: Peter Ustinov; Maggie Smith; Diana Rigg; James Mason;
    Dennis Quilley.

1984 *Ordeal by Innocence*
Source: the novel of the same name
Director: Desmond Davis
Screenplay: Alexander Stuart
Stars: Donald Sutherland; Faye Dunaway; Sarah Miles; Christopher
    Plummer; Diana Quick; Ian McShane.

Television versions have not been included, since they mostly range from
the unconvincing to the beneath contempt. An exception is the recent BBC
series of four Miss Marple novels, with Joan Hickson in the main role.

DISCARD